THEY CALLED ME QUEER

Compiled by Kim Windvogel and
Kelly-Eve Koopman

KWELA BOOKS

Kwela Books,
an imprint of NB Publishers,
a division of Media24 Boeke (Pty) Ltd,
40 Heerengracht, Cape Town, South Africa
www.kwela.com

Cover design: Wilna Combrinck
Cover image of Piper Laurie: Kewpie Collection/GALA Queer Archives

Originally printed in South Africa
ISBN: 978-0-7957-0917-3 (First edition, first impression 2019)
LSiPOD: 978-0-7957-0965-4 (Second edition, first impression 2019)

ISBN: 978-0-7957-0918-0 (epub)
ISBN: 978-0-7957-0919-7 (mobi)

Contents

Foreword

The idea for this book came about while I was in New York for the Commission on the Status of Women at the United Nations. There, I met a dear friend who was in the process of publishing a book in their home country called *She Called Me Woman: Nigeria's Queer Women Speak* – a collection of stories and interviews with queer women from Nigeria. I didn't tell them then, but I had been interested in compiling one for some time too and called on Kelly-Eve Koopman to assist in the process.

In South Africa, same-sex conduct and freedom to any gender identity and expression has been encrypted into our utopian constitution. However, fourteen years later, we continue to fight against the beast of heteropatriarchy that was brought on by colonisation and keeps South African Queer people on the margins of society, usually accompanied by the slogan: 'Homosexuality is un-African'.

The narrative of the Lesbian, Gay, Bisexual, Transgender, Queer, Intersex, Asexual + (LGBTQIA+) community in South Africa has been, for the most part, whitewashed, often excluding the lived experiences of Queer People of Colour (QPOC) who played an intrinsic part in the movement that ultimately brought about the queer agenda of South Africans to various commissions at the

United Nations and the leaders of the African National Congress (ANC) at the time. On an international level, our country has done some incredible things – our policies strive to be inclusive, but what is inclusivity in theory when our very identities are still persecuted by strangers on the street, family members, police officers, teachers, medical staff, pastors, politicians and by the greater society? Therefore, this first compilation of *They Called Me Queer* intentionally centres the writing and stories of QPOC – where freedom was given to be expressive in whatever format brought the contributors joy.

QPOC's stories, when included, usually revolve around extreme trauma. Although this is a reality for most of us as we face disproportionate rates of violent attacks and are more likely to have a lack of access to resources, we are multifaceted humans and we wanted to create a book that portrays that. We have stories of love, we have stories of heartbreak, we have stories of lust, we have stories of resistance, we have stories of being awkward, we have stories of family and acceptance, we have stories of family and rejection, we have stories of self-love and we have stories of people just trying to figure things out.

This book was compiled with a lot of hard work, laughter, community, love and dedication. We hope to grow the *They Called Me Queer* family with each compilation, we hope to include stories from all walks of life, and we hope you learn from reading its pages.

Queerest Regards,
Kim Windvogel

Weight

Shelley Barry

I'm carrying my wheelchair
like a boulder slung over my back
only it's not
it's my wheelchair
and I don't need it in my dream
but I carry it just in case
like I carry you
even when My Back Bends
I'm going to put you down someday
like the wheelchair on my back
I still need to leave this dream
with empty hands

∽

Shelley Barry is a writer and film director, living between Johannesburg and Nelson Mandela Bay. She teaches film at the University of Johannesburg and is the founder and director of the production
company, twospinningwheels. Her first collection of poetry, *The Travelling Poet*, was published by the British Council in 2011.

Becoming: The Fourth Stage
Haji Mohamed Dawjee

Cancer has four stages.

And so does coming to terms with your identity.

Well, in my case at least.

Tomboy was a term thrown around loosely when I was younger. I wore shorts and jeans a lot. I loved Converse All Stars, or any kind of sneakers in fact, and I preferred cutting the hair of my 'passed down' Barbie Dolls rather than playing dress up with them. I didn't mind the term and I didn't need any time to figure out what it meant. But as I got older, I wanted answers. Why was the name Tom in there, what did it really mean, and why was it followed by boy instead of girl? Why couldn't I be a tomgirl instead, if in fact I was just a girl who liked 'acting' like a Tom? Tom, after all, is what we call a boy cat anyway, right?

This is what language does. It evolves. It sits in the Broca's area, the front seat of your brain, slightly to the left, and as you grow it grows with you. It starts to process things as you start to process who you are. And this was stage one. The processing of it all.

My research didn't take very long. The Oxford dictionary gave me a short and simple meaning: a tomboy is a young girl who enjoys activities and games that are traditionally considered to be for boys. Granted, it wasn't everything my heart desired for what, in my mind, was a complex, layered question. But with Google still an underdeveloped, in-the-back-of-someone's-brain ovary, it had to suffice, and suffice it did.

I welcomed the term openly. I didn't notice that it was tinged with the colour of criticism, like being a tomboy was a bad thing. If any negative perceptions did exist, I pushed them away with the facts of the matter. And those were: being a tomboy is cool. It means I get to play outside, kick a ball, shoot an odd BB gun and climb trees. It's fun and what's wrong with fun? It beats watching the boys play while the girls sit on the stoep learning how to cross and uncross their legs on the bench.

But later, the boy part bothered me again. I didn't only like wearing 'streetwear', so to speak. When I was about thirteen, I learned that I really, really enjoyed watching *Sex and the City* and I really, really enjoyed fashion. I was into the shoes, the dresses and the shirts with no pants. I was even into the jewellery. The only thing that didn't quite take was the handbag fascination. I still don't get it. I keep my good ideas in my thought-bag. I don't need a clutch for that.

This was the second stage. What did all this mean then? Was I still a tomboy if I enjoyed high fashion? This didn't quite seem to fit with what the Oxford dictionary told me. It also didn't seem to fit with the views of society. Would everyone be calling me a tomboy if I dressed more like Carrie Bradshaw? The thing is though, as much as I loved it, I really didn't want to, except on the odd special occasion. It just wasn't conducive to my lifestyle or my body image issues. I lacked the confidence to carry off Carrie. And on the odd occasion when I did, like Eid, for example, the tomboy remarks were replaced with something much worse. They were replaced with lengthy statements and interrogations on who I was and who I was trying to be, followed by suffocating gasps of 'Oh my God, Haji is in a dress' or 'I didn't know you owned any girls' clothes (*clutches pearls*).' Of course, at this point my Broca's area was still too underdeveloped to respond with the apposite: bitch, I can wear whatever I want and I don't owe you an explanation.

To this day, one of my favourite secret behaviours is making fashion Pinterest boards. I even eventually ended up buying a really tacky coffee-table book with all of Carrie's clothes and how to wear them plus how the costume designers reused stuff for different outfits. I am a pocket of on-fleek fashion just waiting to burst with a wealth of information. For example, I can tell you that there's a studded, black Chanel belt that Carrie wears in the first film that features in at least three scenes with three different outfits. What do you say? What do you know?

Broca's area intact and severely underdeveloped, I moved on and dragged my identity along at snail's pace until high school introduced me to this idea of being gay and my language centre found itself in the jumble sale of clothes, where fashion goes to die. Is gay the same as being a tomboy? Is that why everyone found it so funny when they called me that? If I am a tomboy, does that make me gay? I swear to God, nothing fucks you up more than a frontal lobe. Enter stage three.

The questions persisted, and the answers fired back: I am definitely NOT gay. I just play girls' cricket, that's all, and tennis as well. I love sport and being active. Are these things synonymous with being gay? 'We can't possibly live in such a simplistic, obtuse world,' I thought to myself as I searched for my cricket whites the same way I searched for myself in the lost and found bin – with both haste and . . . hesitation.

I liked boys. I didn't have any boyfriends at school. The white-school-brown-girl thing made it really difficult, but that's a story for another day. But boys, I did like. I liked them after school and on internet relay chats and on the road when I walked to and from piano lessons. I liked them on SMS and Mxit and, eventually, I liked them on the streets of Laudium on a Saturday afternoon when it was 'bakery hour' and the youths took a single street to drive up and down and check each other out. And they liked me. Are your teens where the tomboy years expire? Will the name-calling stop because I have proved that it doesn't matter what I wear, boys still find me incredibly attractive and I get all the amazing catcalls? Music to my damn ears, I thought with simmering joy.

When things simmer, bubbles form, they rise to the top and then, just like that, they explode. All this happens at great heat and when I hit stage four, that's exactly where I found myself, in a melting pot of fear beyond the bliss of bubbles. Stage four had me stripped down to my naked self. Unarmed as the day I was born. Palms facing the sky ready to receive and knees exposed, ready for falling and grazing. I use the palms metaphor intentionally. Because there's another situation in which some humans have their palms open and facing upwards – when they pray. Or when Muslims pray, to be specific. And Muslim I was.

My dad always used to say the reason we pray with our hands open instead of closed like the Hindus or Christians is because when our hands face us, we in turn are forced to face what they have done, good or bad. And also, of course, they are open in offering and open for receiving. Little did I know that this gesture of worship would close in on me so hard and so fast that faith would find me hands-in-head instead of in prayer and gratitude.

My Broca's area stirred so heavily that it fell to the ground loaded with questions the language of Islam had no way to answer. I spoke to God but he didn't speak back. Maybe it's because he thought I was an idiot and asking him if 'being gay is okay' had an answer I already knew. Denial is the worst sin of all in Islam. Denying God. Denying his word. Denying his existence. Then how, how could I deny I was gay? How could this kind of denying lead me into the pits of hell where I would burn with other bodies who had done much worse? (I had to assume being gay was not the worst crime in God's eyes.) How could who I love give God the right to serve me with the same punishment as he did the thieves and the paedophiles and the liars? If lying was a sin in itself, then how could I lie to myself? Was the road to heaven paved with the self-denial of one's own sexuality?

I read. I read and read and read. And just like that, my dominant hemisphere found the words to produce answers. There is no sin of homosexuality in Islam. The only incarnation of being gay that exists in the text of the Quran is the story of Lut and his people. And the sin is not men sleeping with men. The sin is one of rape, pillaging and the unkind treatment of guests and strangers. The very first word in the Quran is 'read'. And so I did. I read until my eyes bled with information. I read until I disconnected who I was from what I was told religion was and from what I was told being Muslim looks like. I read until I discovered that people are to be feared more than God. And I read until I could disconnect myself from the words of men, the words of God, and the words of history and time and science and fact. Common sense told me that it was impossible for a religious people who existed since the time of Muhammad (the year 570) to not have any trace of a sexuality other than heteronormativity. I dived into the deep end of Rumi, the only evidence of same-sex love I could find at the time. I swam in his love for Shams, his older spiritual companion[1].

I pored over their hours together, cozily talking about love and poetry and music. The thought of eroticism never crossed my mind because it didn't matter. Theirs was a spiritual love that lived its life on pages of poetry, which we still recite at weddings or in love letters. I found stories of Shams disappearing with other men for years on end, leaving Rumi to find new male companions like Salah and Hosam. Did all of this make God love Rumi less? Does all of this make people love him less? And herein was the question of all questions. Was I looking for God to accept me or was I looking for the acceptance of my people? And, most significantly, did it really matter?

---

1   Rumi, J. 1676. *Rumi's Shams of Tabriz (Classics of World Spirituality)*. Vega Books.

My Broca's area is developed enough to communicate this to you now: no, it does not. It does not matter.

The fourth stage of my identity was and is metastatic. It spread with an agency of its own. An agency composed of more answers than questions. It paid attention to alternative meanings and messages. My identity found a home in every cell of my body, the tomboy cell, the cell that likes fashion, the cell that loves sport and the cells that paid attention to what I consumed, and how I fed myself in order to survive. Just like cancer, it took hold of every part of my being until I became.

And I am still becoming.

$\sim$

Haji Mohamed Dawjee is a South African columnist, disruptor of the peace and the author of *Sorry, Not Sorry: Experiences of a Brown Woman in a White South Africa*. Follow her on Twitter and Instagram: @sage_of_absurd

Eating Fried Chicken While Poking My Penis: A Contemplation of Gender
Lyle Lackay

'Are you a boy or a girl?' the Filipino taxi driver asked as I began to cross the busy main road of the small town of Puerto Princesa on the island of Palawan – just one of the 2 000 islands that make up the nation of the Philippines. It was humid. Sweat soaked my underpants and dripped down my inner thighs causing them to stick together. None of the surrounding ATMs would give me cash. Annoyed, I walked back to my hotel with my Jollibee Chickenjoy in hand. I wasn't in the mood for any nonsense – Filipino taxi driver included.

After considering my options, I decided to reply.

'I'm a boy.'

'Oh, well you're beautiful,' the taxi driver said before going back about his business.

Pleasantly shook and a little flattered, I thought to myself, 'If this Filipino taxi driver in a remote island town in the Philippines could be so chilled about gender, what the fuck was the rest of the world's problem?'

They say that Jollibee is the McDonalds of the Philippines. However, the only thing these two giants of fast food perhaps have in common is that you can find a Jollibee at each pillar, post and corner of the friendly nation of the Philippines. And one of the most striking differences between the two eateries is that Jollibee does a divine, coated deep-fried chicken, aptly named Chickenjoy.

Back in my hotel room, as I unwrapped my Chickenjoy – sinking my teeth into the golden crispy exterior and washing each mouthful down with a warm G & T – I looked at myself in the mirror: I'm a gay boy. My personal style is androgynous. My clothes wouldn't raise any eyebrows if they were worn in exactly the same way by either a girl or a boy. But with my hair being longer than it's ever been before, I could almost understand why I was now, quite regularly in fact, being mistaken for a girl – both in the Philippines and back home in South Africa.

A Penis and Cupid's Bow Lips

But still, I wasn't completely satisfied. I took a closer look at my naked body in the mirror: I enjoy my muscular legs and the stature and strength my broad shoulders lend. I love my penis and the fun things it can do and the places it can go. I prize my ability to be competitive, display physical strength, aggression, violence, and other attributes that society so highly values. But just like I possess the physical and emotional qualities traditionally assigned to men, I have feminine ones too – like my pouty cupid's bow-shaped lips, high cheekbones, fine clavicles, rounded hips – and a capacity for empathy, sensitivity, nurturing and other attributes that society so desperately needs. They say you never know until you take a walk in someone else's shoes. And being mistaken for a woman at times, for whatever reason, has given me the unique opportunity to do just this.

When you're a woman, or get mistaken for one, men will offer to do silly, stupid little things for you, like open doors. You'll get many 'after-yous' when either boarding or disembarking an airplane. They will do things I only thought happened in movies, like offering to carry your shopping to your car. But as I most recently discovered, that's not all men do when you're a woman or they mistake you for one. There are also the long languid stares. The unyielding looks that say, 'In this moment, I don't care whether you see me looking at you or not. I will stare until I have my fill. After all, what's the harm – I'm just having a look.' But as women know, and I've come to learn, *a look isn't just a look* – often it's intrusive, annoying at times, and at moments can even instil a sense of fear. Say what you want about those gays, at least they know to break a stare when it's not being reciprocated.

Oh, and then there was that time a man followed me around the supermarket trying to corner me in every aisle. 'Hold on, but what if he knew you were a boy and he was just gay himself?' you may be asking at this point. Well, for gay men, the act of cruising is a skilled and subtle art. What this man was doing was anything but artful. He was definitely straight. A messy, straight man who then followed me all the way home in the dark. 'Fuck this,' I said as I puffed my chest, deepened my voice, and turned on my male gait.

'Hey, fuck the fuck off dude!' I shouted at the man who then sheepishly retreated.

Turning masculinity on and off is something I've consciously and subconsciously mastered and employed many times over the years. Like the other time when me and my gays were down at the hipster bar having a gay ol' time. A skateboarder bro approached and dropped the 'faggot' bomb. Without skipping a beat, I once again puffed my chest, deepened my voice, and cocked my head to the side. The words, 'I will break your jaw', came from my mouth as I lunged forward. In hindsight, even if the bouncer didn't act like a human shield, I wouldn't have actually hit the bro. I merely wanted him to know that I could – threatening behaviour 101. Tapping into some sort of created concept of masculine behaviour isn't a survival trick many women and certain gay men possess. And, at times, this exact thought has moved me to consider hosting a workshop for 'girls and gays' called *How to Fight Toxic Masculinity by Finding Your Inner Toxic Man*.

But then I realise that perhaps we'd all be better served focusing on more important issues. In my age spectrum on the millennial scale, growing up we were either 'straight', 'gay' or 'lesbian' – very few other words existed. So, you either tried to fit into one of these narrow parameters, or you were left wondering, at times confused – becoming more emotionally and physically isolated from your peers. But now it almost seems silly how something as complicated, dynamic, and deeply nuanced as sexuality or gender could be pigeonholed into just three categories. But those were different times, and we made do with what we had. Many years later, just as I started my first advertising gig at Ogilvy, my friend Alix asked if I might be Gender Fluid. Her request came via an email, which included an urban dictionary definition of the term. I had never heard this term before, but it sounded right. It felt good. I've always liked the word 'fluid'. It denotes an openness – a feeling of flexibility. A freedom to move. A freedom to be.

Joy

I finished the last of my golden, crunchy Jollibee Chickenjoy. It was a thigh – I always save the thigh for last. I finished a quarter bottle of gin while watching a lovely show about Filipino beauty queens. By now the slow, dull, tropical Filipino heat was causing the walls of my hotel room to close in on me. A little drunk, I slipped on my orange swim shorts (which were actually just girls' jogging shorts), threw on a flowing, rainbow-striped kimono and headed down to the pool.

'Good evening, ma'am', the pool bar waiter smiled as he greeted me. I ordered a San Miguel Pale Pilsen and took off my kimono. Only wearing my shorts, I jumped in the pool. The pool bar waiter approached and, as he bent to hand me the San Miguel, he kindly said, 'Your beer, sir.'

∽

Lyle Lackay is a copywriter from nine to five. And an essayist the rest of the time. Find them on Instagram: @lylechristolackay

Harnessing the Power of Queerness
Lwando Scott

When I was in grade four, my mother and I were walking a family member, a distant aunt, to the bus stop and just before we arrived at the bus stop, my aunt asked my mother if she wasn't scared of 'Satanism'. This was code for homosexuality. This is just one of the many times that I would endure wounding statements coming from people throughout my young years. When I was growing up, queerness was often framed as a lack, a loss, a deficiency, a state of being that needed alteration, cleansing, and praying over. This was first evident in the ways that adults spoke about my effeminate behaviour in my presence, sometimes with coded language, as if I wasn't there. I was visibly queer at a very young age, where other people told me that I was queer – often using the most derogatory language – before I could even articulate that queerness for myself. This meant that in my young years, I associated my queerness with derision. While effeminate embodiment and intonations in a boy do not necessarily mean homosexuality, they do raise suspicion, and in my case, it was true that I did have romantic desires for other boys, even as I concealed these desires. The game of avoiding detection starts the minute you leave home, as everyone you encounter is a potential threat armed with pejorative statements. The irony of me always trying to avoid detection was that it was almost impossible to hide, as everything I was pointed to my otherness. What was jarring about my attempt at concealment was how impossible it was to conceal who I was because it was almost always visible. It was in my walk, it was in my voice, in the way I expressed myself with my hands, how I preferred the company of women to that of other men, and how I envied all my girl friends who could go to home economics while I had to attend woodwork. It was a period in my schooling years I dreaded and had to endure. For many of us, the process of discovering our sexuality is further complicated by our non-conforming gender identity and gender performance. When you are an effeminate boy, it is other people who first impose a gay sexual identity on you before you have actually discovered it for yourself. The linking of 'effeminate' behaviour or mannerisms in boys to same-sex desire or attraction is misguided of course because there are plenty of men who are effeminate or have 'girly' mannerisms or are considered soft but are heterosexual. When you are a queer young boy, the name-calling creates all kinds of confusion because before you have 'weird' feelings for boys, you are already demonised. By the time I was starting to have feelings towards other boys as a teenager, I was already bruised and dealing with feelings of shame. The feelings of shame only intensify with the teenage years. You fall in love with boys around you at school but nobody knows except yourself. You are also afraid of being discovered, so you don't stare for too long but, of course, you are already discovered.

Growing up queer in South Africa was to experience an unnerving feeling of a desire to belong and that desire never being met. With everything in my life, or so it seemed, I was doomed to exist on the periphery. Like many queer kids, I knew there was something eccentric about me. Growing up as a gender nonconforming young boy, in other words growing up as an effeminate boy, I felt the brutal brunt of sanctions for being this way. I carried the burden of always trying to avoid detection because the teasing, name-calling, and sometimes violence was a real threat. In hindsight, after reading many social science books written post World War II, I was able to understand what was happening to me. Two scholars come to mind when I think about my young self and the trouble I went through, albeit often in vain, to avoid detection that I was queer. I think of the concept of stigma that was conceptualised by Erving Goffman[2], and how those who possess a stigma, in my case my queerness, will go to great lengths to hide that stigma so that they are not prosecuted for having said stigma. When I think of the way I would walk around wanting to be invisible at times to avoid detection, I behaved like someone who had a stigmatised identity, and this caused me great shame. Another writer who has subsequently helped me think about my young self is Michel Foucault with his ideas on discipline[3]. Foucault argues that we are disciplined in society through many techniques and so we

2   Goffman, E. 1963. *Stigma: Notes on the Management of Spoiled Identity*. Penguin: London.

3   Foucault, M. 1991. *Discipline and Punish: The Birth of the Prison*. Penguin: London.

modify ourselves to fit into the status quo, to fit in, to be seen as normal. In my attempts to avoid detection, I was being disciplined by South African society because the threat of mocking, of name-calling, and of physical violence was enough to make me try and conform to avoid detection.

Shame became a part of how I experienced myself. There was a feeling of shame surrounding my 'failed' masculinity and later on there would be a shame as I felt an attraction to other men. The shame I felt for being effeminate and the femmephobia I experienced because of my girly ways was the initial prejudice I experienced. While growing up, at times, it felt like there was no greater sin, greater betrayal of your 'own' kind, than deserting masculinity for femininity. The gender shame I felt as an effeminate boy was complex in that there was already shame attached to *how* I was even before I knew *what* I was and what I *desired*. This was most pronounced in men-only spaces as masculine hierarchies were enforced, like in the woodwork classroom. Shame is a feeling that followed me for a long time and remains a feeling I have to struggle against as it never completely leaves you. It creeps up on you when you are mocked by someone for your gender non-conformity. Shame rears its ugly head when you realise that even other gay men are femmephobic and that in trying to find love, I have had to navigate a world of 'Masc 4 Masc' and 'No Femmes'. The rigidity of normative gender ideals in South African society meant that no one escaped unscathed, including those, or maybe particularly, those who were themselves escaping prosecution. The production of shame while growing up didn't only affect me. I saw how it affected those around me as well. Although it was never said, there were some family members who displayed feelings of shame towards me because of my femme behaviour. Shame is complex; it is like a disease that spreads to those around you and they in turn deal with it in their own ways. Its manifestations are often unpredictable. Shame can be all encompassing, but it can also be certain aspects of yourself that produce it or are affected by it. Often, we do not know what to do with feelings of shame. It is like a hot coal you drop immediately once you realise what it is, but it might already have burnt you. I would cope by extricating myself from those who induced shame in me and also those who were embarrassed by my shame. This means that I found peace in my own company with my thoughts. When we grow up queer, even as we deny it, we have no way of embracing that queerness because we grow up in intolerant environments. When we are queer, we know, perhaps even instinctively at first, that queerness is evil and it is something you will figuratively and literally be punished for, and so you learn not to embrace that side of yourself. When you are queer and you know it, your attraction to boys paralyses you and instead of embracing the feelings, you push them, you fight them, you might even punish yourself for them. This is usually particularly the case if you grow up in a religious environment. At other times you embrace the feelings for boys but they are often experienced in solitude. Especially when you are still trying to figure out what you are feeling and why you are feeling this way, while everyone around is feeling differently than you, as in feeling 'normal'. The discovery of yourself and your sexuality is a fraught process regardless, but it is with added complexity when you are attracted to people of the same sex.

Thinking back on my younger years, there were contradictions with regards to my queerness and how I was navigating South African society. I was a happy-go-lucky boy who loved beautiful things and my flamboyant personality ran up against the sanctions I would endure for being a happy girly boy. It was also this happy-go-lucky disposition that endeared me to many people, mostly girls and women, but also some men, very few men. I remember a family friend telling me that she couldn't feel that I was an only child because although I was, I was open and embraced others as if I was used to having siblings. When my happy-go-lucky disposition was met with femmephobia and homophobia, I mostly retreated although there were times when I fought back. So I would vacillate between self-imposed isolation and my happy-go-lucky self. I knew the isolation was part survival because hell was other people, and so, being by myself meant that I wouldn't be victimised. Little did I know that my queer-come-flamboyant personality would one day be an asset in creating wonderful relationships with people from different corners of the world and providing me with incredible tools to question normativity in South African society. That it would be my queer disposition that would attract me to sociology, particularly diversity studies, where I learned about difference and how difference matters and how difference affects people's positions in society. Ultimately, it is because of my own queerness and the myriad of other experiences linked to race, class and gender that I pursued an academic life. A life of trying to make sense of myself and articulating it to the world, and to understanding what difference is and how we can operationalise those differences to create a more inclusive South African society.

As time went by, I started maturing into my queerness, meeting different people, reading queer books, kissing boys, studying sociology, and I started realising that my queerness was in actual fact an advantage. It was, in certain situations, a power that I could harness. It was something I could use both to feel my way through the world but also a tool to question the taken-for-granted structures of my world. My queerness was turning out to be an asset, accumulating worth as I experienced more and accumulated more knowledge. It has enabled me to question things that others take for granted, like ideas around gender and gender performance, as I had first-hand experience in how my gender had been policed throughout my life. My queerness enables me to see the world differently compared to many of my contemporaries who are heterosexual but also those who are cisgender homosexual. Being queer enables me to imagine a different world where alternative genders and sexualities are not things to be policed, judged and demonised but are to be embraced, encouraged and explored. Queerness was a starting point of imagination, of fostering different ideas of how to be in the world and what it meant to exist in it. I realise that queerness was the opening up of the world, where I pondered: what is normal?

In this piece, I am inspired to reflect on my queerness and the treasures that have been offered to me through queerness. I am inspired because although I struggled coming into my own through shame and self-doubt, I can't imagine my life without my queerness. It is feeling, doing, living with and through queerness that I feel in touch with my humanity and that I am striving to live the best life possible, a life characterised by desire in all its different manifestations.

The ideas around the formation of my queer identity come from a long list of phenomenal people who have charted a way for many of us through writing about queerness. I am indebted to many people in the fashioning of my identity, including my mother, my girl friends in high school, my queer friends throughout my university years, and my lovers. All of whom I hope to write about one day. Here, though, I speak about those people who wrote about queerness and made me see myself. The way they articulated queerness liberated me and gave me a language to talk about myself and the future world I want to be part of. Although I have spoken about myself as a gender non-conforming, queer femme boy, queerness encompasses so much more than that. My disposition, my identities, my gender performance, my queer identity, my desire for other men – I am only a part of the cosmos of queerness that exists in South Africa and indeed, Africa. My ideas about queerness have been heavily shaped by the queer scholars who critiqued the normative ideas around gender and sexuality. I was influenced by the words of Michael Warner when he said that, 'The preference for "queer" represents, among other things, an aggressive impulse of generalisation; it rejects a minoritising logic of toleration or simple political interest-representation in favour of a more thorough resistance to regimes of the normal.'[4] I was struck by the 'resistance to regimes of the

---

4   Warner, M. 1993. Introduction. In, *Fear of a Queer Planet: Queer Politics and Social Theory*. University of Minnesota Press: Minnesota.

normal' because I knew very well what he meant as I had first-hand experience of being regulated by being told that I was not normal. This was profound for me and how I saw my life and where my life could go. It was a statement at once describing how my life had been and also called me into action to resist the power of the norm. To resist the idea that I am a loss or deficient by questioning the very logic that constructs what is normal and what is not normal. To this Michael Warner further argued that 'if queers, incessantly told to alter their "behaviour", can be understood as protesting not just the normal behaviour of the social but the *idea* of normal behaviour, they will bring scepticism to the methodologies founded on that idea.' This gave me the knowledge and therefore the power to question the gender and sexuality hierarchies inherent in the world around me. The questioning of such hierarchies remains at the forefront of my work, academic and otherwise.

Reading queer theory made me think about myself in different ways. It made me hopeful about the future and because I began to see all the ways we could deconstruct gender and sexuality, I began to imagine ways we could undo and redo our normative assumptions about gender and sexuality. This idea of a different future, a future with alternative genders and sexualities was captured in David Halperin's assertions about queerness as an 'identity without an essence, not a given condition but a horizon of possibility.'[5] This was an amazing thing to read because

5   Halperin, D. 1997. *Saint Foucault: Towards a Gay Hagiography*. Oxford University Press: Oxford.

it stretched my thinking. Here I was told that my queerness contains within it a horizon of possibility. To me, David Halperin was alerting us to the endless power of queer imagining and that we will not arrive at some destination and say we have achieved 'queerness' but that the process of trying to reach a state of utmost queerness is itself the magic. To be queer is to inhabit a forever open state of being, in other words, gender and sexuality are not static entities but are constantly moving. David Halperin's articulations are closely linked to those of José Muñoz whose writing moved me to the point of tears because it was beautiful and so affirming of my identities. José Muñoz describes queerness eloquently and beautifully as follows: 'Queerness is not yet here. Queerness is an ideality. Put another way, we are not yet queer, but we can feel it as the warm illumination of a horizon imbued with potentiality. We have never been queer, yet queerness exists for us as an ideality that can be distilled from the past and used to imagine a future. The future is queerness's domain.'[6] The beauty and liberation offered by the assertions from José Muñoz can only be understood in the context of pushing against restrictive ideas about what is possible for queer people in a world dominated by heteronormative structures. His assertions are a refusal that queerness can be caged or said to belong to one entity or time period but is an ever-moving idea.

Clearly, reading queer writers played a large role in shaping the way I see myself, my gender and my sexuality. They were instru-

_____

6 Muñoz, J. E. 2009. *Cruising Utopia: The Then and There of Queer Futurity*. New York University Press: New York.

mental in how I began to see the power of my queerness and how in many ways it was that power that many people feared. These writers taught me to tap into that queer power and use queerness as a tool to think. They wrote in order to harness the power of queerness within me to help me embrace myself and perhaps even change the world, particularly with regards to gender and sexuality. Reading was fundamental to my growth as a queer person. In many ways the world of books has been my saviour because when I was lonely and running away from the hard and homophobic world, I sought refuge in books. It is also through the enjoyment and the power of books that I am writing this story to be part of a larger volume of stories of what it means to be queer in South Africa at this juncture.

Growing up, who would have thought that thinking about gender and sexuality would become such a big part of my life; I am using the very things that were once used to shame me for empowerment and changing the world around me. Queerness and reading about it have led me to academia. I am currently waiting for my PhD thesis results from external examiners. My PhD is on same-sex marriage in South Africa and it was inspired by the queer theorists I name in this piece, as they were the ones who laid the foundation in helping me think critically about normativity. My PhD research focuses on the aftermath of the legalisation of same-sex couples and how couples are making sense of what it means to be married in South Africa. These questions are important if we consider that same-sex couples can legally marry in South Africa but violent crimes against LGBTI people remains a concern.

Like most black South Africans, I grew up in a township and it was in Port Elizabeth. Like most South Africans, I have a difficult relationship with race as a construct, a concept and an identity because of the history of apartheid and the residue of that history. My racial identity is made even more complicated by the complex ways it intersects with my sexual and gender identities. There is a die-hard narrative in South Africa, and other parts of the African continent, that homosexuality is 'un-African'. This is a narrative that posits same-sex desire as something that was taught or learned from European settlers when they invaded parts of Africa. What this narrative negates is the existence of same-sex desire in many different communities in different parts of the continent with different meanings that at times have nothing to do with the notion of 'gay' as understood in the Euro-American imagination. The narrative of same-sex desire as 'un-African' is built on the rejection of imperialism but does not take into account that anti-sodomy laws in all of Africa were the product of settler colonialism laws created to discipline the 'native' because African cultural practices were a foreign concept to the European mind. In this then, there is a need to decolonise sexuality and how it is constructed as part of imperialism even though it has been part of African culture for centuries.

In my struggle with the intersection of my race and sexual identity, I found solace in the words of Simon Nkoli. Simon Nkoli was a pioneering figure in the building of the South African sexual liberation movement. He was a black man and he was at the forefront of both the struggle against apartheid and the struggle for sexual liberation. Through the Gays and Lesbians of the Witswatersrand (GLOW), Simon Nkoli, Bev Ditsie and others organised South Africa's first gay pride march and Simon Nkoli captured the salient intersection of race and sexuality at the march when he said, 'I am black and I am gay. I cannot separate the two parts of me into secondary or primary struggles. In South Africa, I am oppressed because I am a black man and I am oppressed because I am a gay man. So, when I fight for my freedom I must fight against both oppressions . . . All those who believe in a democratic South Africa must fight against all oppression, all intolerance, all injustice.' To see myself like this was life changing. He encapsulated what I had felt for a long time but was unable to verbalise. The racial identity of Simon Nkoli mattered as it affected how he experienced the world. His queer identity also mattered because it was how he desired in the world. In post-apartheid South Africa, while race is generally understood as a social category, sexuality remains illegible to most people. The life of Simon Nkoli was a light for black queer kids like me: to see myself represented in a figure who looks like me, who walks like me, who talks like me and who loves like me. Simon Nkoli was a hero, he was a beacon of light, he represented that 'queer horizon of possibility' and the queer 'ideality' of the future, and I am that future. In turn I must do my part to create possibilities and idealities for other black queer kids so they can imagine themselves way beyond my existence. Now I see Simon Nkoli as belonging to the ancestral realm, I see him as a guiding spirit that looks on us and sometimes marvels at the seeds he sowed and how they have sprung up and will further seed for future generations of black queer kids.

When I think about my queerness, both in the gender non-conforming sense and my sexual identity, and then I think about the impact of race on my life, I can't help but think of the many ways that colonisation and then apartheid impacted my life. The social, economic and psychological impacts of these histories cannot be overestimated. Colonisation and then apartheid took away black people's right to selfhood, self-determination and the freedom to self-discover. The end of apartheid in 1994, the introduction of the South African Constitution in 1996, and then the legalisation of same-sex marriage in 2006 are all opportunities for South Africans to craft themselves. In the post-apartheid period, we are given free reign to craft ourselves and that crafting includes the crafting of a sexual self. Colonisation and apartheid took away black people's ability to create themselves in ways they desired. In many ways then, queer people are great examples of the freedoms offered by post-apartheid South Africa. In fact, they are living embodiments of the possibilities contained in this glorious post-liberation moment in South Africa's history. As a country, we would do well to applaud and take lessons in how *to do* freedom from queer black South Africans. While far from perfect, I am a product of post-apartheid South Africa, and when I consider the constraints that my mother's generation had to endure and fight against, I owe it to them to craft the most liberated queer self possible.

The evolution of my queerness has not ceased. Like all people, throughout my life I have gone through changes. I think my twenties were the years that I became radicalised in my thinking because of the exposure to amazing thinkers at university.

Now that I am in my early thirties, I have a renewed sense of appreciation of myself and my sexuality. In 2017, a tweet by @Introvertgay went viral. In the tweet, @Introvertgay said, 'Gay culture is being a teenager when you're 30 because your teenage years were not yours to live.' The tweet went viral and caused much debate about what it means to grow up gay with many others chiming in about their experiences. I have since been thinking about this tweet, why it resonated with many people and how it spoke to me. The tweet made me think critically about my own journey as a queer person in my early thirties. For many reasons, when you are younger you do not have the independence, economically and psychologically perhaps, to embrace the kind of queer person you see yourself to be. There is also the age factor, that you are much older and much more matured and so you are more able to embrace yourself. Though I am convinced that the major reasons I feel so much stronger in my queerness in my thirties than before is because I embrace my queerness. It is hard to embrace one's queerness in your teens because you are trying to run away from it in most cases, even the most camp amongst us. I have had conversations with my queer friends about turning 30 and how we feel so much more at ease with our queer identities after struggling with these identities in our teenage years and for the better part of our twenties. I enjoy my sexuality so much more now than when I was younger. There has been something particular about turning 30 for me, maybe this is what everyone experiences, I don't know. I like my queer self, I am basking in my queerness and embrace the idiosyncratic parts of my gender performance and my sexuality. I am becoming the queer I never knew I could be but realising the potential of this queer me has always been there.

The tweet shared by @Introvertgay became such a sensation because in less than 140 characters, he captures the first 30 years of many queer people's lives. So, turning 30 and feeling and behaving like a teenager is really speaking to the freedom that you have at 30 that was impossible when you were having crushes on people of the same sex when you were sixteen. In turning 30, I am more confident in my sexual identity, and I can go to queer spaces and meet other queer people who see me and understand me. I can inhabit queer spaces where I can make friends and meet potential lovers without fear of being 'caught' or physically assaulted. I enjoy sex. My friends and I have discussed just how much we feel comfortable in our sexuality and how we are willing to experiment with our bodies. In my early twenties, it was hard to even be honest about what I wanted sexually because to state your desires was to be vulnerable to judgement and shame. Now, I embrace the particularity of my sexual proclivities. I embrace the hungers of my body, my heart and my head.

In South Africa, there is an enormous demand to conform. Even as people come out as lesbian, gay, bisexual and transgender, there is a tacit (and sometimes explicit) demand that people embrace the normative straight culture at the expense of queerness and queer culture. The demands to be included in institutions like marriage are part of the desire to be part of straight culture and to be cloaked by the veil of normality. I am not suggesting that queer people do not deserve social justice and to have their rights respected but the form these rights take must be placed under inspection. As a queer person, I shouldn't need to be like, act like, love like, have sex like or desire like heterosexuals or adopt heterosexual culture in order to be seen as human. I am enough as a queer being. Being queer has taught me that we sacrifice the greatest parts of ourselves to belong and we never stop to ask why there are heteronormative demands in order to belong. Why is belonging, whether it is to belong to South Africa, to the male fraternity, to family, hinged on adopting heteronormativity? When I look back at my life, I have rebelled against heteronormativity and its demands all my life, even when I didn't know I was doing it. I refused gender and sexual categories even as I struggled with feelings of shame; my queer spirit was defiant to the calls to be normal and delivered a fulfilling queer life. I hope that this essay can be a demonstration of the power of queerness. That just like José Muñoz once quipped, the glory of queerness is yet to come[7] for many black, queer South Africans. By this I mean that I am a beginning, the seed, a light that lights a thousand other candles in someone else's imagining of their queer self. I am excited when I imagine queer African futures. I can't contain my excitement when I think of the many ways we haven't even imagined the potential of queerness in this beautiful country and, indeed, this continent. In looking back at my own journey, I am amazed at what this continent can produce because my queerness is a product of this country and continent. Now, when I think about my young self and how defiant I was of normativity, I can't help but chuckle

---

7   Muñoz, J. E. 2009. *Cruising Utopia: The Then and There of Queer Futurity*. New York University Press: New York.

and think of how society punished me for it – but that boy defies you still.

~

Lwando Scott is post-doctoral fellow at the Centre for Humanities Research at the University of the Western Cape. Lwando's doctoral thesis is on same-sex marriage in South Africa and is titled *The more you stretch them, the more they grow: Same-sex marriage and the wrestle with heteronormativity.*

Tyron's Prayer
Lester Walbrugh

If he is going to do it, he must just do it and get it over with.

His mother has her boys, him and Hilton. And Hilton has his *tik*. Tyron does not want *tik*. He does not want anything everyone else has. He wants his own thing, his own life outside of what he feels has been given to him. He would never have chosen this for himself. But now, if anything, and with his options exhausted, he realises that he has a choice.

Hilton has stayed out all day. It is dinnertime and his mother is frantic with worry. She calls Tyron into the kitchen.

'Do you know where your brother is?'

'No.'

'Tyron. Tell me now. Does your brother *tik*?'

'I don't know, *Mammie*.'

'I am going to ask you one more time. Does. Your. Brother. *Tik*?'

'I don't know, *Mammie*.'

'Fine. I just hope you know that if there was a chance that we could help your brother, then that chance is over now. You know you are the only one who can save him. Other than our Lord and Saviour and our prayers, and God knows I have run out of them, I do not know who can help him but you, Tyron. You're his brother and if anyone knows him better, then it is you. And if you say Hilton doesn't *tik*, then I must just believe it. I will pray to the Lord and direct my prayers to whatever can be wrong with my child. I believe you, Tyron. I always believe you because you will never lie to your mother. You respect your mother as you come from a good Christian home. You know what is right and what is wrong because you have been cleansed in the holy water of Christ our Lord, who will keep us and provide for us.'

His mother turns to her faith whenever she is feeling hopeless. It does not happen often but when it does and she is like this, as if in a trance, it frightens Tyron. His mother grabs his wrist and drags him to her bedroom.

'We have to go on our knees, Tyron. Let us get to our knees and pray. Let us pray for your brother. Let us pray for you.'

Tyron says, 'Amen,' as he was taught to do ever since he could speak.

The room is stuffy. The curtains are closed. There is a gloom in the air and it smells like talcum powder. Underneath it all, there is a sourness. In the past few months, his mother has rarely left her bedroom. She spends days in bed in what Tyron can only describe as a kind of stupor, either sleeping or about to drift off. Scattered on the bedside table and on her dresser against the wall are magazines and newspapers and Game and Shoprite pamphlets, papers torn and papers written on in her illegible hand. Careful circles in faint ink mark discounts on everything from pool equipment to hi-fi systems, a vacuum cleaner, a new lounge suite with dark, expensive-looking wood, and a washing machine.

They are dreams of things she will never have, of a life where she would need these things, and of a life with lots of space, a husband and shiny, new sons who do not *tik* or who, in the corner of their room when the lights have gone out, do not lust after men. These things are a chance to start over and for his mother to have the life she deserved.

And she deserves all of that, Tyron thinks. She does. His mother deserves the best but all she has is them. He feels sorry for her. His sympathy for her is stuck in his throat, and it grows with every prayer of hers, from every call for help she sends up and out into the darkness. If you love something, set them free, he thinks. She might not love her prayers, but she loves them, her children, and must set them free. If she is unable to do it, he must set himself free from her and show her that he can make his own decisions. He chokes and coughs into his hand.

'The Lord has said, "Go and praise the name of the Lord." Know that he cares for you and will provide for you, especially when your path is dark and narrow. It is then that he will be by your side.'

(Breathe! Praise be to God! Everything will be ok. I am blessed and I am protected by the word of the Lord.)

'Let them see, my Lord. Let them see the error of their ways and lead them to salvation, my Lord Jesus Christ. Those who deny your word, let them see, as you have shown me. As you have opened my eyes to the truth, my Lord. Let Hilton find his way home tonight. Let your light guide him through the dark streets to find solace and the everlasting love of Jesus Christ, our Lord. Let my son know that he is not alone and that he is worthy of love, my Lord and Saviour.'

(The light of the Lord will guide me. Whatever I do, whatever I am – this thing – there is salvation for me. Our Lord is merciful.)

'And the Lord will look after you, my son. The Lord will reach into your soul and grab the illness there that has been eating at you, my son.'

(Go! Go now and satisfy this urge that will drive you mad if you don't!)

'And my son, Tyron, I know he has a difficult time, my Lord. But you only give the difficult times to the ones you know are strong, my Lord. The ones you have given the strength to deal with whatever comes their way, my Lord. With the evil and the unjust. With the devil and the hatred so many live with within their hearts, my Lord. You have made my son pure and in your image. He is blessed beyond and I can only thank you, my Lord Jesus Christ, my Saviour."

(He will protect me. He will love me.)

'As we walk in the valley of the shadow of death, my Lord, do not forsake us.'

(Amen.)

∽

Lester Walbrugh is from Grabouw in the Western Cape. His short fiction is in Short.Sharp.Stories's *Die Laughing*, Short Story Day Africa's *ID* and *New Contrast* magazine.

Beads

Shelley Barry

my spine/wounded
jutting
raised
your hands flutter on my skin
i pull you inside myself like a tortoise
your whisper thrills as you say
my bones-
feel like beads
decorating my back.

~

Shelley Barry is a writer and film director, living between Johannesburg and Nelson Mandela Bay. She teaches film at the University of Johannesburg and is the founder and director of the production company,
twospinningwheels. Her first collection of poetry, *The Travelling Poet*,
was published by the British Council in 2011

Three Crows Before the Rainbow

Katlego K Kolanyane-Kesupile

The sun cracked open the flower buds in the garden as a shrill strum of the blades of grass shrugged dew drops to the soil. Morning was Duchess's favourite time of day when she was younger. Somewhere between coming back from the escape of dreams and knowing that she was safe before others became a part of yet another day, she treasured lying in bed and listening to nature greet its timekeeper.

'Children of the desert know its melodies before they can name them,' her grandmother used to say. The very same croak of a frog which now riddled her with anxiety used to delight her younger self – through this she knew the rains had fallen leaving puddles to be jumped in. As a child, she would sooner scale a mopane tree than watch television, much to the displeasure of every mother in the family. With her cousins, she'd make race cars of sun-dried ox tailbones and rate the amount of fun had on an afternoon by the number of new scars lining her legs.

Adding years to her age had twisted the story of this desert princess who'd now opt for a hunt in a mall over one in the wilderness she'd grown up navigating. The bush she now inhabited as a varsity student was Johannesburg – city of lights, money and debauchery. A young, lithe seductress of her own making, she knew she had her pickings in a place where the hunters and the prey often switched places at the snap of a manicured finger. Duchess took particular pleasure in how you could disappear in a room full of people in this city. She didn't quite know when this kind of being alone started feeling like morning.

She had taken a fast liking to the brilliant city, its infamy lingering in the back of her mind but not stopping her from matching its shine. You'd have to strain your imagination to trace this city slicker to humble, cattle post beginnings. It alarmed her friends, at first, how Duchess managed to look like she was working a catwalk regardless of the time of day. The long limbs which had speedily carried her across many finish lines in her youth were now envied for a different reason. An infamous thrifter, balling on a budget was both a means of survival on her tight student budget and the key to honing her signature eccentric, yet classic, style.

Thero had first seen Duchess at a department meeting and, being her senior, wasn't surprised by what he thought to be yet another attention-seeking freshman. His world was completely rattled when chatter among his peers revealed that she was, in fact, from the same sleepy country of Botswana that he came from.

'Did you say she's from there or her family comes from there?' he chirped, trying to mask his disbelief.

While he didn't know her from a spore in mud, he felt a strange wave of nausea wash over him. A knot formed in his gut as his throat dried up, his mouth refused to flood with spit and his jaw became achingly tight. That day, he watched her like a dog watches its master cutting meat for drying. She, on the other hand, continued to flitter about from one chatty group to another, oblivious, much like a bird, of her watcher.

*

'Are you particularly fond of him?'

The words crept past her ears and, noticing her lack of reaction, the middle-aged white woman repeated herself – her tone bobbing between placating and reprimanding.

'Are you particularly fond of Kgosi?'

'I don't understand what that means, ma'am. We're peers and friends. I have no reason to not like him.'

'That is not what I am saying. Teachers are concerned. We've noticed that you two are very familiar with each other.'

'Because we talk and hug in the corridors?' She choked back a chortle which would have most certainly expressed her indignation.

'Amongst other things . . . yes. You know the school rules and you two present something which could become very tricky if we are not careful.' The straw-haired woman rose to her feet feeling the teenager's sharp, feline gaze locked on her. In some way, she too was in disbelief that she was betraying the tenets of the school culture that the student sitting in her office had been an exceptional embodiment of.

The deputy head averted her eyes and said, 'We've never stopped you from hugging the girls who are your friends, right? But if we are to ensure that lines aren't blurred between other boys and girls in this school, as seniors, we'll need you and Kgosi to limit your physical contact.'

*

A waft of the smell of warm bodies and cigarette smoke smacked her back into the crawling line. Some new bouncers had been hired and the police crackdown in the buzzing streets of Melville had them staging this masquerade, lest they risk losing their gig. This being her final year of varsity, she'd been a regular patron for some time – enough time to render any debate about her looks and her documentation null. However, the flash of that memory in the deputy head's office suddenly made this line an all-too-familiar scenario – was she 'girly enough' to be deemed worthy of the protection of men, or would today be another day when she'd be asked to pay cover charge?

A moment before her card was called for, a glint of fake gold hanging from a thick wrist called her attention to a hand stretched out to her. Sizwe nodded to the equally beefy men sitting at the door and pulled Duchess through. She smiled and nodded at the men while letting a sigh get drowned by the music. The pair walked through the gyrating bodies with Sizwe's grip steering her by the hips. He was a lover of nice things, so the dreadlocked, statuesque nubian goddess in skin-tight ripped jeans, studded combat boots and a graphic T-shirt draping off her shoulder was a fitting complement. They had only just sat down when a Joe Budden song sent their neighbours flying out of their seats, coursing past Thero, who had a Long Island Ice Tea and two Heinekens in hand.

'Here you go, princess,' said Thero, handing the cocktail over.

'Thanks, babes,' replied the youngest of the group, exchanging winks with Thero.

Sharing Sizwe, and the magic of time, had changed Duchess and Thero from being unconnected country folk into being confidants. They had become more like cousins than friends. Sizwe, a former high school rugby player who had earned national colours and was the current assistant coach of the varsity team, struck up a friendship with Duchess when he discovered her equally successful athletic past. Rugby had now come to replace basketball as what she pokingly called the 'girlfriend sport' on her social calendar – building her network beyond the queer kids and theatre crowd. When Thero's star began to rise on the team, Duchess inadvertently became a regular feature in his life with the two seeing each other in the drama department hallways, on match days and at team braais – where she'd still flitter about entertaining players' partners and yapping with the boys about the season. It had been at one of these socials a year ago when Thero's first true impression of her had been unknowingly revealed to Duchess by one of his Batswana friends.

The drama department was sufficiently small enough for all five of the Batswana enrolled as students to be forced to know one another. Much to his displeasure, there wasn't a single person with anything bad to say about Duchess. She had a way of winning people over with her no-bullshit approach to celebrating her life. His one thought continued to be how unnatural an occurrence she was to him – too free to come from a culture that had entrenched in him what boys could and definitely should be. She was like staring into a glaring noon sun – hot and blinding.

*

'I'd denied you to a number of people actually,' he had said, with shame, as he drove her home after a celebratory night out with Sizwe.

'I'd like to say I would have expected better from you but you've already set honesty as the only option in this conversation now, haven't you?' she quipped before launching into her effervescent laugh. 'The thing with secrets is that they become as heavy as an elephant when you start to care.'

Years of confronting the restrictions of masculinity and toying with gender at drama school had softened the rugby player's ego and he had learned in his own quiet way how to submit to himself without hiding behind his culture. As the car stood still in front of the men's residential hall she had been assigned a room in, the irony of the scene had never been more poignant to the two of them.

She stepped out and asked him, 'You've had two years, so do you claim me now?'

'Do I have any other option?' replied the young man before watching her walk in.

Chivalry wouldn't let him drive off, though he knew she'd saunter past the guys at the entryway without a care. He waited for the light to shine through her window; she waved and blew him a kiss as she drew her curtains closed.

*

The hallways were abuzz with people chasing after the luggage trolley, dropping off their room keys and preparing to abandon the residence hall. It was the fourth winter she'd lain in bed listening to these sounds of the morning. She let out a hearty sigh as a smile took over her face. It was only a matter of time before one of her 'boys' – as she called them – would come knocking on the door to say his farewell as if to a maternal figure. These were young men from far-off villages in the east and north-west of South Africa – places where only a fortunate few would drive themselves to, in lieu of mounting a rickety bus with crying babies and squawking chickens.

Duchess's partiality to storytelling over a drink – a tradition she'd learned from uncles and herdsmen with her cousins back in Botswana – had made her assimilation into a few of the boys' spaces she'd wanted to hang around much smoother. There she was no less queer, nor any more of a villager. In this city of lights, football banter during the World Cup and rally song chanting in the stadium stood side by side with vogueing on balconies and scouring racks for the most fabulous fashion finds. The young teenager who had been told to set a better example by not hugging boys in corridors had charged her spirit with the electricity of Jozi *maboneng* and formed a star.

For Thero, who was now a post-graduate student, the morning broke and he too packed up his things to make his way back home to Botswana. This would be another winter where he'd feel brave enough to not deny the link he shared with Duchess when he got home. Another winter where her name would slip into conversations to which his friends would ask when they'd get to meet her.

Missing her, he would call to check in and she would swiftly affirm that everything was alright before rattling off in her usual way. He'd anxiously wait for a moment to see her break out in all her colours again, upon their return from a country full of sleepwalkers who didn't know how to smile at a rainbow like her. He would never deny that she had given him new eyes, and helped chart a new path for his life driven by bravery and kindness.

'Think of me like Jesus and Maya Angelou,' she'd once said to him. 'You can deny me three times before the good ol' cock crows but this bitch is still gonna rise!'

~

Katlego K Kolanyane-Kesupile is a performance artist, musician, writer and LGBT activist from Botswana. She was Botswana's first openly trans-identifying public figure. Follow her on Instagram: @katkkolkes

Open Letter

Craig Lucas

Trigger warning: suicide

This is an update of an open letter I posted to social media at the start of 2016. I had been deeply unhappy for such a long time. I hit rock bottom on 15 January 2016. I was at work thinking about how I'd nearly flung myself out the train that morning. I'd been thinking about suicide a lot. It scared me. Suicide and mental illness run in my family, especially amongst the men. My dad committed suicide when I was three. A number of other close family members tried too – some succeeded, some didn't. I hadn't felt alive in a very long time. Is this what they'd felt like before they decided to put a gun to their head? The death of my father planted a seed in my mind. Those seeds had sprouted like flowers over a grave. I spent many years denying a big part of myself. I carried my shame and my self-hatred around like a rotting limb. The rot was spreading and it was killing me. I didn't want to die. I swore I would never be like my father. I would never put my mother through that again.

Thank God for rock bottom. Everything became clear and I knew that I needed to let go of all the shame and all the pain I'd been harbouring. And I did, and I was free. Two years later though, I found myself back there. I'll explain.

Let me start a couple years back – December 2011 to be exact. I remember coming home one night. I'd been out drinking. It was late. My mother messaged me to say that they weren't home and that she had hidden the key in the usual spot. It took every ounce of strength in me to keep my body from caving in on the way home. I managed to make it just past the kitchen before falling to the floor. I prayed. I screamed. I cursed. I prayed some more. I should probably backtrack a little more. You see, I'd spent that day out drinking with a friend – someone I met during my first year at UCT. We had most of our philosophy lectures together. We became very good friends over a very short period of time. We were extremely close – best friends even. We'd go out to drink often. We'd get drunk and talk about anything and everything. It was his birthday that day. It wasn't supposed to be any different to the other times, except for the fact that we'd probably just get a little more drunk than usual. But that day wasn't like all the other times.

There was a pervading energy at our little corner table that I hadn't felt before. I felt slightly tense. I could tell that he did too. Our conversations started to get deeper with every drink. Stares lingered just a bit longer than normal, our seats moved closer, and time seemed to slow down with every shot of whiskey. I found myself fixated on his eyes and his nose and on his lips – the way his top lip curved like the ebb and flow of the ocean, how the creases danced over the skin like folds on a rose. His lips parted and then met with every word he said like the wings of an eagle in flight – virile but tender, crude but graceful. I was so enamoured that often I didn't even hear what he was saying, but it didn't matter. All that mattered in that moment was that he was there and that I was there with him. That was the moment it hit me – I was in love. I was unequivocally, profoundly, violently in love. I was unequivocally, profoundly, violently in love with a man. My head started spinning and I felt like I wanted to throw up. I made up an excuse to get home. I couldn't get out of there fast enough.

You see, the problem was that I had dated girls before, and I was sure that I loved them. I'd had sex with girls before and I knew that I'd enjoyed it. What I was feeling didn't make any sense. I'd never been more terrified in my life. I cut all contact with him. I spent the subsequent three years in a perpetual state of war with myself. It took me four years to accept what happened that day.

On 15 January 2016, I shared my story with my friends and family. I was free. I found love for myself again, and love found me. Then came *The Voice South Africa*. People started telling me to keep the fact that I was in a relationship with a man a secret. 'The audience is conservative,' they said, and 'No one will vote for you'.

So I did, and I won.

'I'm glad I listened to them,' I thought.

People then said, 'No one will buy your music if they think you're gay,' and 'Girls are your biggest market, you will alienate them'.

Before I knew it, I was right back in the closet again.

It's been one year since I won *The Voice South Africa*. My dreams had come true. I was in a relationship with an amazing man. My career was flourishing. I was wholly depressed. Suicidal thoughts plagued my mind. I'd become a very angry man. Hurt people really do hurt people. I hated myself. I was wasted every other day. There were even drugs. I'd forgotten myself. I'd forgotten that I was smart, talented, funny and kind. I'd forgotten that I was loved. It took me hitting rock bottom once more to realise that I'd been living a lie. Now, more than ever, I have so much to live for, and I want to live.

My skies have been grey and cloudy for way too long; a cloud is only allowed to become so heavy before it bursts and rain comes falling from the sky. I'm ready for that rain to come and wash away the sadness that has been tainting my mind and my heart for the last two years. I'm ready for the rain to water my gardens and give life to the seeds of joy that I know lie very deep within my soul.

I don't know what's going to happen next. I expect to lose a couple of friends and fans, and I expect a couple of familial relationships to become strained as a result of this letter, but it's okay. I sing about 'Hearts Exposed' but hid mine. So here I am pulling my best Frank Ocean. I welcome whatever is coming my way with an open heart and an open mind. Until then, I have some making up to do with the people who stuck by my side, even when I was at my worst, and some amazing fucking songs to write.

Love only,
Craig

Craig Lucas, from Elsies River in Cape Town, is a graduate in Economics and Politics from the University of Cape Town. But despite a promising career ahead of him in the corporate world, Craig secretly loved singing. He was the winner of the second season of *The Voice South Africa* in 2017 and signed a record deal with Universal Music immediately afterwards. His debut single, 'I Said This', reached number one on iTunes within a matter of days, and his debut album, 'Restless', was nominated for a South African Music Award.

Questions Asked
Sandrine Mpazayabo

I entered the cab hurriedly, trying to appear as apologetic as I could for causing the driver to wait so long. He called once while I was still putting on my shoes and again as I was trying to get myself to stop crying and face the day that lay ahead of me. As I closed the door behind me and we sped off to work (I was already twenty minutes late and unfortunately had to make it his problem too), I shut my eyes, trying to keep myself composed. My voice trembled as I asked him to raise the volume of the radio, and even though the music blasting from the speaker was offensively bad, I hoped it would distract him from his distraught passenger.

'Where're you from, sister?' He eventually asked, seemingly not noticing the fact that I had been sniffing and wiping my eyes for the past few minutes and so was clearly not in the mood for small talk.

'Uhm,' I said, not at all taken aback by the question (the previous day I had been asked the question four times, the day before that seven) but rather astounded, as though someone had shaken me awake from a deep sleep. I coughed and blew my nose, unable to produce a coherent sentence just yet. The driver, unbothered by the state I was in and determined to get an answer, continued.

'I mean, on the phone I was convinced that you are South African. You have that accent a lot of Capetonians your age do. But now, looking at you, I get a completely different impression.'

I sighed.

He grinned. 'Can I guess what you are?' I stared ahead and blinked. 'I'm thinking Kenyan. No? Ugandan. Nigerian? Wait – Ethiopian? Hold on . . .'

I cursed loudly and said, 'How come I can only be one?'

The driver, stunned, started a sentence but I didn't let him finish. Normally, I would calmly answer that my parents came from Rwanda, but I was born and raised in Cape Town, and then redirect the conversation to what the ethnicity and nationality of the driver is and what languages they spoke. Otherwise, the conversation would almost immediately revert to Rwanda's painful history and/or the reasons behind my possession of refugee status despite the fact that I was born in this country and had never been anywhere else – both matters which I had run out of strength to explore. However, after the shitstorm of the morning I had had, and the fact that I would have to fake politeness to a bunch of strangers for the next eight hours in the second-hand clothing store I worked at, I just felt like being candid for a moment.

'You cannot just simplify my identity like that.' He began to speak. Fired up, I cut him off again. 'I know you don't mean harm and I usually don't mind that whole conversation. I'm having a bad day that's most likely not going to get much better so I have no energy for this right now.'

We were both silent. He had muted the radio while speaking earlier so now the only audible sounds were the mild flirtations of the wind outside, the GPS voice and his fingers uncomfortably tapping the steering wheel. I knew I had already kicked over the pot, so I decided to break the silence.

'I was born and raised in Cape Town. Hence the accent or whatever,' I said, sounding like a primary school pupil reciting an oral presentation their mother had forced them to practise for hours. 'My parents fled Rwanda in the nineties.' He nodded slowly. The silence stung. Although I had given him a healthy piece of my mind, I felt even more defeated than when I had first entered the cab. I turned to face out the window and didn't bother to wipe the tears that followed.

*

I have lived my entire life squeezing between binaries, climbing over them, slowly shuffling through the narrow passages between 'here' and 'there', 'this' and 'that'. A square peg, the most rehearsed element of my existence has been uncomfortably forcing myself into round holes, in and out, in and out, in and out, but mostly in. Never belonging is –

'Excuse me? Young lady?'

It was a thick Afrikaans accent that pulled me out of my head. I blinked hard, trying to orientate myself. It was a few hours after the cab incident and I was zoning out behind the counter of the empty store. The person standing before me had sun-bleached white skin, a shock of white hair, an unsettlingly wide smile and a loose khaki shirt which matched his too-short khaki shorts. He was holding two equally horrendous shirts – one was a dull orange formal shirt and the other a faded green T-shirt. He held them both out and then put each to his chest.

'Which one looks better?' he asked in a volume much too loud given he was the only customer in the store.

It took a lot out of me not to say 'neither', so I pretended to analyse each one closely. 'What's the occasion?'

'A braai with friends. Someone I like will be there and I want to dress to impress.'

'Hmm.' I walked around the counter and down an aisle which had a variety of decent looking large shirts. I selected about three and gave them to him. 'You'll have to try these on for size, but I think they're much nicer than those two. Although if you really want to get one of those two, the orange one suits you better.'

'Ah, thanks,' he said, cradling a heap of shirts in his arms. 'I'll try them all on and see which I like best.'

It's a sinking feeling. It's heavy, it lags behind you, bouncing around on the floor, tethered to a string you're inescapably attached to. I wonder whether other people feel it too, whether they wake up every morning under a pile of bricks and run through familiar but frightening forests before they fall asleep every night. The sun-bleached hands slammed a R200 note on the counter, bringing me back into the real world again. While I was doing the transaction (he ended up buying the terrible orange shirt), the unsettling smile and the eyes above it stayed on me.

As I nervously printed the receipt and bagged the shirt, he cleared his throat and asked, 'So do you and your boyfriend ever go to braais?'

I didn't bother to conceal the annoyance in my voice. 'I don't have a boyfriend.'

I knew that was the wrong thing to say because he put his bag and receipt down and rested his hands on the counter, ready to investigate my statement.

'No man in your life? Seriously?' his smile reminded me of some super villain whose name I couldn't quite place in the moment.

'I . . . I am not interested in men at the moment.' I stared longingly at the door, hoping a customer would put me out of my misery.

'What does that mean?'

'It means that I'm not interested in men at the moment.'

His uncomprehending look made me want to scream. It was one I had seen too many times.

'I like men and women. Sometimes I only like men, sometimes only women. Sometimes both. It's just how I am.'

I shrugged and shimmied past him to my saviour, an obviously lost passer-by standing outside the shop, looking around the street in confusion. As I was directing the person outside to the coffee shop they were looking for, I saw the man walk out of the shop and to his car. I sighed, feeling defeated once again.

This can't be life, this can't be life. Life could never make sense. It simply couldn't. Nothing was simple about it. I chuckled internally at this daily thought. Am I South African? No, but yes. Am I Rwandan? No, but yes. My queer identity felt like an even more layered question. I struggled with placing myself, locating my position, and relating to others. I struggled to belong, to identify with, and to be certain in something. There were so many questions that needed answering and I felt totally out of my depth. The uncertainty was initially stifling but would begin to feel comfortable, even liberating, as though I was concurrently a blank canvas and a passionate artist. The realisation fell into my lap while I was leaning against the shop door, smoking my post-shitty-shift cigarette and watching the sun tuck itself neatly behind the mountain.

Two people, ostensibly a couple having an argument, walked past me. 'You don't have to have an answer for everything, James,' the one person said loudly, shaking their head in irritation.

That statement hit me hard. Obviously having a far more profound effect on me than James, who simply cursed and said something about feeling so damn fed up about arguing all the time. I threw my backpack over my shoulder and walked towards the taxi stop, feeling, for the first time in much too long, grounded within myself. You don't have to have an answer for everything.

The answer to many of my questions: some things just are. I was one of them.

∽

Sandrine Mpazayabo is a writer, aspiring professor, DJ, and creative enthusiast currently completing her honours in African Studies at the University of Cape Town. Born and raised in Cape Town but classified as a refugee, Sandrine has always been passionate about social justice issues.

Trans-Afro-Futurism
Clio Koopman

Stephanie, my best friend, and Kristen, my girlfriend, stand around me stuffing my *tette* (tits) into a sports bra then my binder then bandages. I imagine myself as a trans anti-apartheid activist. I imagine myself as a trans slave. I am not only myself in 2019. I am myself in these identities. I have lived through slavery, colonialism and apartheid. My body has been sold, commodified, controlled and eventually set free. All this happened while being trans. Time starts and ends with trauma and our trauma is the moment when our lives start and end. We experience trauma every day and this is how time ticks by.

Kristen told me I looked handsome, my mother told me I'm a patriarch, a guy on the street called out to me '*my bru*' (my brother), I got asked how I suddenly decided to be a man, and people at work misgendered me. Every day my existence is experienced and subjectified differently. Every place I go to experiences me differently and every hour my existence changes.

I am not pedantic about pronouns or about changing names mainly because I know I will become the ridicule of friends and family. They would whisper derogatory thoughts through the grapevine of all that connects us, and they will do it secretly, not overtly, because everyone in my life is supposedly 'woke' and fear being dragged by the rest of the 'woke police'.

Through this writing, I want to explore what it means to be trans: what the word means, what it looked like in the past when the Dutch met the Khoi and when the French Revolution happened and when it was World War I. I want to explore myself as if I were in those situations and look at who I could've been when Stalin came into power, when Jan van Riebeeck colonised us, and when Nelson Mandela walked out of his cell. How would I have responded to those events through my trans-ness and what was my place in them?

I also want to explore what my trans-ness could look like in the future when technology takes over, when black people reign and when medicine allows us to live forever. What will my trans-ness look like in the future? Will it be different? Or will it stay the same? What's really important when I start thinking about my identity and my trans-ness is when I start to think about the words and language we use. If enough people say the same word, only then does the word take on meaning. I read a quote that said: 'Words identify us with trauma that is not our own.' This is so powerful when thinking about the word 'transgender'. We, as trans people, see and read that word and can feel our past lives, our ancestors and our identities that existed before it was a word. We read it and we also connect it to our future trauma that is yet to come, already written out.

Trans: the prefix meaning 'across', 'beyond', 'through' or 'changing thoroughly'.

Transportation, transformation, translucent.

All these words are magical as the meaning of the prefix gives rise to meanings of movement. I like to believe this is because trans people have moved through time and space. We have always existed and always will. Being trans is magic. I fear I am fetishising the trans experience and narrowing it down by association to a word but words are important, history is important, and the future is important. We exist through all these things: words, history and the future.

Let me set the scene – we're in the 1960s. Stephen Bantu Biko walks into a dimly lit basement. PAC and ANC manifestos are scattered around the room. Black men smoke cigarettes and drink beer, and the air smells like resistance and rebellion. As he walks in, everyone's attention steers away from the conversation they're having about black consciousness because the man himself has arrived – Biko, the thinker, the activist, the rebel. Under his corduroy jeans, his pad starts to feel heavy and his cramps worsen when he has to pretend. He carefully shifts his binder. No one can know. The nurses that give him his testosterone shot at the clinic signed a contract of secrecy and are slipped money for 'cooldrink' every time he comes. Biko is the poster child of masculinity and of what a strong black man is. No one can know he has a vagina, breasts and menstruates.

Why is this so ridiculously hard to believe – that one can be trans when having to fight for one's blackness, life and freedom? Why can't we comprehend that oppression doesn't only have to be one thing. The scenario I set sounds like feminist bullshit. How dare we give privilege to an issue like gender when people were dying at the hands of the white apartheid government. Let's continue to imagine Biko and his pad and his binder and how uncomfortable he is while he has to fight. Why can't we imagine a struggle where gender issues completely intersect with race issues? Truth is, we don't have to imagine that. Black trans people are the most oppressed in society. Which oppressive factor comes first is not important. There is no such thing as a more important oppressive factor.

For fear of sounding like the University of Cape Town gender studies drop out / trans activist / feminist I am, I acknowledge the anger that some people feel towards the growing importance of gender and queer rights and how it is considered a luxury while people are killed for their ethnicity and starving because of their class. I also acknowledge that my imagining of the trans identity might be essentialist and idealist but it is how I imagine trans to be and my personal experience, so I think it's okay.

Picture it: the year is 3035 and black trans people run the world. Genitals have been bred out, babies have consciousness and are taught the teachings of Kimberlé Crenshaw, bell hooks, Audre Lorde and Winnie Mandela. The ruler of the world is a trans non-binary person who was chosen to rule because of their superpowers, allowing them to understand even the most complicated of intersectional theories.

This is what my knee-jerk response was to imagining a trans future. I am disturbed by how Westernised my conception of the future is, even though it is black and trans. Why are American feminists' teachings what the babies learn? I don't even know of any African black trans people to take their place because we are not represented, heard or seen in the way we need, and often are made either hyper-visible or invisible. We are either reduced to stereotypes or over-analysed. Our bodies are either fetishised or illegal.

Perhaps the future is a place where I'm trans and my identity isn't theorised or understood through a Western, white lens. A future where we as black, African trans people are able to create our own words and meanings for what it means to be trans.

While I write this, all of me is tired of having to constantly validate my existence, of shielding questions about who I am, of doubting who I am, and of struggling with acceptance.

I base my life and my activism on three factors: history, language and future. I look to history to define myself and understand where I fit in. I think about Steve Biko's pad and Robert Sobukwe's binder as I navigate the world. I dream of carving out futures where we are not seen as anomalies, not seen as characters or abstract, alternative figures who are looking for attention or trying to add to our pain by 'choosing' this path for ourselves. I also look forward to a future where there is no hierarchy of the trans experience, where I, a trans person who still wears eyeliner sometimes and asks my girlfriend to open the mayonnaise jar, is still seen to be as much of a man as someone who has undergone top surgery or gender reassignment surgery and hangs out with boys on the weekend, watching soccer and drinking beer.

I dream of changing language and of creating new words for words that are tied to colonial, Western concepts of gender. I want a new word to describe myself. I am myself in the past when I was sold and commodified. I am myself in the future when I come out to my grandparents and they speak proudly of my bravery at church to aunty Minnie and uncle Cyril. I am myself in the future when I don't worry about what people think of me, about how trans I am or if I am judged for the way I love, dress and present.

I live knowing how proud Winnie would be of me, how proud Oprah and Kewpie and Laverne would be. I fight every day for my past and my future. Life starts and ends with trauma. Life is healing and learning. I am constantly on the path to healing through every interaction and everything I do. When I wash my body, I think of how I am cleaning away the dirt – the dirt of rape and abuse, the dirt of violence, and the dirt of the past. When I cook my rice, I think of myself being sold or bartered for rice. When I choose my outfit, I think of the hands that were exploited to make my Nike T-shirt. I cannot separate myself from the trauma my body has gone through, both through time and the future. Simultaneously, I cannot separate my triumphs from those who have gone before me and those who will come after me.

I transcend. I transform. I translate. I do my trans-ness every day.

Viva to trans Steve Biko! Viva to trans Sarah Baartman! Viva to trans Nomzamo! And viva to me!

~

Clio Koopman is a young trans man originally from Cape Town. He completed two years of a Bachelor of Social Sciences at the University of

Cape Town, majoring in Gender Studies and Anthropology, and is currently completing his degree through the University of South Africa. He lives with bipolar syndrome and is an activist, a campaigner, a writer, a fighter and a lover.

The 'Yes' Ice Cream

Carl Collison

Trigger warning: sexual violence and rape

His slim, delicate fingers handed me an ice cream. I knew his story, he knew. He knew who I was, I knew. But we had never met.

In that tacky fast food joint where he was slogging away earning a pittance in that dry-as-fuck rural town, he handed me an ice cream. It was his way of saying 'yes'. Yes to me, the helicopter journo from the Big Bad City wanting a piece of him. His story.

But it was weeks later – the Yes Ice Cream long forgotten – when he finally allowed me in. Allowed me to tell the dark story they – those farcically entitled thugs – had forced him to make, forever, part of his own.

Gang-raped – not once, but twice – they made it known how much they hated him. Him, the *'moffie-naaier* (faggot-fucker)'. Him, the soft-spoken young man with the tiny frame, the soft eyes and those beautiful, slim hands. The hands that had given me the Yes Ice Cream.

Hands that had tried – pointlessly, as the men forcefully, repeatedly entered him – to plead 'no'. Hands that had tried to fight them off, flitting desperately between clawing furiously at them and mutely, feverishly pleading a simple, desperate 'no'.

Who, though, but the blind can hear mute hands screaming 'no'. They were not blind, the men who hurt him. They saw his hands. They saw the hands of this protesting Strange Fruit. The very same hands that kindly, knowingly, acceded, handing me the Yes Ice Cream. They saw his hands, but did not. Could not. Would not. They did not, after all, know the story. The story of the man who handed me the Yes Ice Cream.

∾

Carl Collison is currently the Other Foundation's Rainbow Fellow at the *Mail & Guardian*. He has contributed to a range of local and international publications, covering art and social justice issues. He is committed to defending and advancing the human rights of the LGBTQI+ community in Southern Africa. Most recently, he was shortlisted for the 2018 Gerald Kraak Award and Anthology, which celebrates excellence in queer writing and photography across Africa. Follow him on Twitter: @carlcollison

Of Names and 'The Blood That Falls'
Carl Collison

Trigger warning: sexual violence and rape

'*My naam?* (My name?)' he asks the audio recorder he clutches in his one able hand, as though it is the device, rather than me, who had asked him. Realising this, he lets out a self-deprecating laugh. Then, in a tone at once self-conscious and proud, he says: '*My naam is Daniel Ivan Thomas. Maar die mense noem my Daantjie* (My name is Daniel Ivan Thomas. But people call me Daantjie.)'

It is a Sunday morning and the smell of the being-prepared weekly feast – boiling beetroot, steaming squash, pan-fried potatoes – wafts through the barely-furnished, two-bedroomed council *huisie* (house) in Tulbagh's predominantly coloured township of Witzenville.

From the threadbare one-seater he sits in, Daantjie tells of how it came to be that, to this day, he still has to deal with '*al die bloed* (all the blood).'

It was five years ago, around 2 am. On his way home from a wedding, and taking a shortcut through '*die wit mense se gebied* (the white people's area)', a kick to his back sent him to the ground. His attacker dragged him to a secluded area a short distance away.

There, he says, '*Hy't my geskop en getrap, sy penis in my mond gedruk en na hy my verkrag het, 'n bottle kop in my in gedruk en 'n stok ook.* (He kicked me so badly, forced his penis into my mouth and, after he raped me, forced a bottle into me and then a stick.)' For added humiliation, Daantjie was pissed on.

'*Meneer, ek het erg geskeer en gebloei* (Sir, I was very badly torn and bled a lot),' he sighs.

'Daantjie's attack was one of the most brutal attacks I've seen,' a gravelly-voiced, seen-it-all activist once told me, frustratedly flicking cigarette ash onto the pavement.

The attack was, of course, made all the more vicious (well, in my mind at least) by the fact that Daantjie stood very little chance of fighting back. You see, since birth, he has only been able to use the left side of his body. Cerebral palsy, the doctors said, once they'd eventually diagnosed it.

You could see it as he sat in that tattered-ass chair, when something as simple as lighting a cigarette took some by-now-used-to co-ordination. But it became very evident when – slowly dragging his one obstinately unresponsive leg behind the other, more-sure-footed one along those dry-as-fuck streets – he took me to where '*die voorval* (the incident)' took place.

'*Dis hier, meneer* (It's here, sir),' he says, pointing out the tiny piece of land adjacent to a bone-dry ravine screaming to be quenched and littered with discarded Shoprite shopping bags and empty plastic Coke bottles. '*Dis hier waar hy my so verkrag het.* (It's here where he raped me like that.)'

Leaning his tiny frame onto a chest-high barbed wire fence (erected by officials with embarrassed haste after he reported the rape with fuck-the-consequences defiance), Daantjie explains how, foiling his desperate attempts at escape, his attacker would, again and again, drag him back to inflict more and more hurt.

Entering him first with his cock.

Then with the bottle.

Then with the stick.

Then to piss on him.

There was blood.

Lots of blood.

Always the blood.

'*En weet jy meneer, ek was 'n maagd* (And you know, sir, I was a virgin),' he says, repeating it several times. '*Ek was 'n maagd . . . 'n maagd.* (I was a virgin . . . a virgin.)' His attacker still walking free, Daantjie is left with little more than the bitter memory. And, of course, '*die bloed wat val* (the blood that falls).'

'*Elke keer as ek 'n nommer twee het, dan is dit net bloed wat afkom* (Every time I do a number two, then it's just blood that comes down),' he says. '*Weet meneer* (You know, sir),' he adds, '*As jy mooi kyk, is dit ons mense wat uitgeroei word, gemoor word, verkrag word, geslat word, doodgemaak word – especially hier by ons in die Witzenberg area.* (If you look closely, you'll see it's our people that are being exterminated, murdered, raped, beaten, killed – especially here in the Witzenberg area.)'

Daantjie knows it could have been so much worse. That he is one of the 'lucky' ones. You see, there were others in that particular rural Western Cape region so rich in fruits and wines, in pain and anguish. Others who have (or, should we say, 'had') names.

Phoebe Titus.

David Olyn.

Jakob Tromp.

Brendon Hufke.

Knifed, raped, dragged to their deaths in empty fields or bustling streets, tortured, set alight – they had names. Names, stories and lives forced, kicking and screaming, to relinquish all to the hate behind that word we all know so well: *'moffie* (faggot)'.

In the years, months, weeks, days, seconds before their untimely end, they were really nothing but *moffies*. *Moffie-naaiers* (faggot-fuckers) deserving of little more than a spit in the face; a knife rammed into the throat; pairs of feet repeatedly stomped on the head; a lit match laughingly put to a petrol-doused body; pieces of plastic pushed into a mouth pleading pointlessly with perpetrators for pity. Their blood caking for a short while, as though in farewell to the soil from which they came.

There were, of course, those who had survived. Like Daantjie, they'd survived. But, he says, *'My wese is van my af. Ek het nie 'n menswese nie . . . My menswaardigheid is weg en hier loop die ou hier. Ek meen, ek is disabled. Ek moet nou permanent hospitaal loop.* (My being has been taken from me . . . My sense of humanity is gone. My dignity is gone and here he is, still walking the streets. I mean, I am disabled. I have to go to hospital permanently now.)'

'En ek bloei baie. Die bloed kom nog altyd af (And I bleed a lot. The blood is still coming down),' he says of the ineffective pills he is being given to stop its unyielding flow. He now uses sanitary pads. *'Soos 'n vrou moet* (Like a woman has to),' he says. *'Of miskien net 'n lappie of iets.* (Or maybe just a piece of cloth or something.)'

The blood will, more than likely, flow from him for a while yet. But it will stop. It will go. But what will not go is this: he has a name. Daniel Ivan Thomas, as he so proudly says it. Daniel Ivan Thomas. They call him Daantjie.

∼

Carl Collison is currently the Other Foundation's Rainbow Fellow at the *Mail & Guardian*. He has contributed to a range of local and international publications, covering art and social justice issues. He is committed to defending and advancing the human rights of the LGBTQI+ community in Southern Africa. Most recently, he was shortlisted for the 2018 Gerald Kraak Award and Anthology, which celebrates excellence in queer writing and photography across Africa. Follow him on Twitter: @carlcollison

String of Advice

Luh Maquba

Pulled from one generation to the next
Thread of knowledge lost in each season
but the similarities return like old fashion
Misunderstood
An Idea of one influential person is worn.
A perfect fit.
Magnificent souls lost in outfits outside the fitting room.

Alone;
A place where no one is given time
to dwell since it causes you to be a misfit in reality.

We are clothed to hide our true selves.

Our identities are locked in documents with names we
abandon behind our parents' backs.
We silently wish upon their death in exchange for freedom.

Our bodies are burdens we didn't choose to carry.
Enlightenment is a risk where knowledge has no place
to bury.

Those who make it are lucky not to return while the struggling are waiting for their turn.

On a thin line ...
We thread.
Still a garment can be made to hide the never-ending despair.

~

Luh Maquba is a photographer and an LGBTQI activist focused on the rights of the marginalised intersex community. Luh resides in Johannesburg. Follow them on Instagram: @lurighter

To Poly or Not to Poly?

Kim Windvogel

Except for the Debussy piano trills coming from the speakers, the atmosphere around the table is rather quiet. We sit in musical silence and then she shows me pictures of her body (pre-babies) and mentions how different she feels, more able yet less capacitated.

'Does that even make sense?' she asks.

'I wouldn't know,' I say, 'but you look the same to me, maybe even better right now.'

I watch her disregard my compliment. What is it about accepting compliments that makes us wilt? What is it about criticism that makes us jump out of our flesh and take note? I am at her house because I need a place to sleep and, to be honest, I wouldn't mind her soft yet assertive company.

The piano in the background is the only sound I can hear other than her infrequent, deep breathing. Her sighs signify that she is clearly not in the mood to work. Neither am I, but I won't interfere. I sit and intentionally feel her energy complain with every intake of air – a clear sign of the need to surrender, but still I say nothing.

Silence doesn't scare me.

I don't know why I decided to come and sleep at her place. Maybe it is the babies, their laughter, their tantrums, their longing to communicate their feelings without crying and I think of how I still struggle with that. Maybe I am just hoping that they will teach me how to do it, like baking scones from scratch or starting and finishing a book in one night – the type of book that haunts you for weeks after you finish its last page – or like watching a flower bloom while marvelling at the thought that you are yet to bloom. Then wondering whether you will ever bloom again, like the day you figured out the difference between 'please' and 'thank you' or the day that you realised that you really are over them.

I don't know. She is clever and damn determined. How else? There are people who depend on her work as a visible, queer Muslim and a believer in the abolishment of prisons. She has a piercing in her right eyebrow and wears a ring that means something in Arabic. I have forgotten what it means. I am forgetful. She will probably realise this if our friendship were to continue. She listens to classical music when she studies and listens to traditional Arabic music when she's dancing with her children. This suits me. I am a classically-trained singer and, after years of hating what I'd studied, I have finally found a use for it – playing music I grew to detest for someone who could teach me how to find joy in it again. That feeling of being a tourist in your own city. That feeling of reigniting a passion.

I go quiet when she speaks. Strange territory for me as speaking is kind of my thing. What was life like in the countries she used to call home – where her family still resides, where war ravaged homes, killed love, and rebuilding is constant? These thoughts come and go and then she suddenly lifts her face from her page and asks me if I know what 'facial sufficiency' means. And I think of my face and how sufficient it would be in her cupped hands, our pouted lips barely touching – maybe just for a second, not sexually but playfully. She laughs, almost like she read my mind and mutters something about lawyers' language and elitism. And I laugh too because well, it's painfully true.

*

She paces up and down and tells me to say stop whenever I'm ready. I frown, because I am curious. She hasn't even touched my body and even if she did, why would I tell her to stop? But I decide to play along and obey her request.

'Stop.'

The word escapes from my mouth and after I ring the command, she suddenly stops pacing and walks towards me with a book in hand, one finger wedged into its sleeves. I wonder how long I have to wait before she does that to me. She opens the book and starts to read from right to left. It's Arabic and, although I do not understand a word she is saying, my clitoris nods in agreement to every sound she's making.

'It's quite difficult to translate. But it's a good one for you,' she says and raises her pierced eyebrow at me. 'You said stop at the right time.'

I impatiently wave away a need for an explanation, while she mutters a short, inaudible translation of a poet and their grapple with life. I pay it little mind. I want her to tell me to say stop again. I want her to insert that finger inside that book's sleeve again and I want my clitoris to nod in agreement with every sound she makes from right to left again. I want to imagine her doing this to me over and over again.

*

The next day she asks me, why am I supposed to make the first move?
Is it because I look like a butch?
No, I replied, I wrote you a short story and it had a title and everything.
Come to think of it, I wrote it by hand
and I think that's a grand move
– kissing is the last piece of the puzzle, I add.
(I mentally curse my incessant need to theorise things before they
    happen)
and then she laughs and says, I don't agree with your kissing com-
    ment . . . Additionally
(lawyer act coming out in role play,
as she removes her glasses,
folds her arms and furrows her brows)
in your short story you said you don't want me to caress you 'sexually,
    but playfully,'
– you were explicit.
Yeah, I laugh, because I was throwing you a curveball.
You're confusing me, she says and places her glasses back on her face.
Anyway, she continues, as she finally turns back to her papers,
    maybe kissing isn't the first move, but it is the most definitive
    move.
Later that day at the same table, she leaned in to kiss me,

83

as our tongues caressed I hoped my lips
were as soft as hers and that my mouth wasn't too dry.

*

She smells like 2005
Musky Axe and Brut and that blue bottle of roll-on my granddad
   used to use
Inhaling Her armpits – long breaths that remind me of days spent
   labouring
Her chest is tilted to the left
I said it was created this way because Her heart
is Her biggest asset and she tells me I was born a pivot to poet
I am equal parts disillusioned and indifferent
by how fast the imagination can create alternate universes
in a matter of days,
in a matter of hours,
in a matter of seconds in which your life is an open ending with
   many doors leading into different rooms depicting various
   versions of your future
I go ahead and open each door to view my options, behind:
Door One: I'm on the phone about my visa, trying to stay without
   consequence
Door Two: she is packing her bags to move to my country without
   consequence
Door Three: I'm boarding a plane and going home in a week as
   planned
Door Four: I'm busy having a threesome with Her and Her friend
   she introduced me to last week

Door Five: we're cuddled together in bed, it looks like a couple
of months have passed and there are Xi'an's takeaway boxes on
the floor
I open door three and walk into its scene, slightly regretting not
taking part in what's behind the reality of door four.

*

What is the difference between throbbing and thrusting, she asked
me one day
and upon seeing my smile, she shyly retaliated, I'm not even English!
And I laughed and said, I wasn't judging
Throbbing comes before and after thrusting, I said
You throb before pleasure, then you throb after pleasure
and she smiled at me
I didn't know if she tricked me into giving that explanation but I
have a weakness for her accent
Does your girlfriend know about me, she asked one morning
Yes. I told her I have a crush on you, I told her I'm going to make a
move on you
that's brave, she said – then I pinned Her to the bed, held Her down,
watched Her struggle to release Her body and felt a surge of
emotion escape my spirit as I collapsed next to Her, laughing,
thinking of nothing in particular, thinking about everything
in particular.

*

It's a sunny day in South Africa.

I have arrived home and she is waiting for me. I am late, the flight was delayed. I tend to fall asleep once boarding a plane and therefore did not let her know that my flight would be delayed by more than an hour. She is visibly irritated, but it quickly subsides.

We are driving, and she says she is happy I am home. I kiss her because I am happy to be with her. The conversation is the same way it has been for the past two and a half years: easy, fun and taking place with our hands intertwined over the gearbox. I casually mention that I touched her, that we fucked. She says nothing for a few minutes. 'I am in no position to make you feel guilty,' she says heavily, without removing her fingers from in between mine.

Being poly in a relationship with someone who is monogamous-leaning is difficult. It creates this tension where there should not be tension. It creates guilt where freedom and love should reign. Being poly does not mean you spread your legs for every person who passes your way and even if you do, that's your consensual business, but this is a misconception. Polyamory means different things for different people. I tend to fall into emotional connections with people and this leads to a physical boundary that, at some point, needs to be crossed. Sometimes that physical boundary does not get crossed and I am okay with that. There should be no question whether we can love more than one person at a time; we are complex and multifaceted beings and loving and lusting two or three people at the same time is possible. So why then, when these are my beliefs, at least for now, do I feel guilty about what I am doing? Why, when I am open and honest, do I feel like a liar?

Have you ever done something by the book and it still airs the same results in the 'post-dealing-with-the-admin-of-emotions' phase? Have you ever taken the yoke off your neck but still felt heaviness around you? Have you ever done something *not* by the book, *not* taken the yoke off your neck but still felt heaviness around you? Those are branch feelings of internalisation. Internalising the need of the world for us to choose that one person – be monogamous – and internalising having to do things, not by your own borrowed and mentally written-down and saved concepts, but by another's? When we internalise things and are aware of it, we have this opportunity to face that feeling, name its existence and figure out what the source of that feeling is and whether to try and fix it or, like many of us do, ignore it.

Not all our internalisations will be because of a partner thinking of polyamory and the other craving monogamy. A lot of them will be because of family members, a lot of them will be because of past traumas, a lot of them will be because of paranoia, a lot of them will be because of religious training and the so-called moral compass, even because of deeply buried resentments.

If you are of colour, you will face them because of your race every time people say things about it without directly saying anything about it (*I know that you know that I know that you know what I am talking about*) or, even better, when they start their sentence with 'I'm not racist, but . . .' (Maybe if you are a woke-white, you will internalise your actions, whether intentional or unintentional, to improve on your colonial background – this is a toss-up.) We will face them because of our genders (if you are a cisgender heterosexual man, maybe you will internalise your actions, whether intentional or unintentional, to improve on your colonial and enforced colonial backgrounds), we will face them because of our geographical locations, our bodies, our friends, our competitors, our sexuality, our cultures, the way we live our lives or what we saw on television!

Most of these internalisations mentioned will be stirred up because of what others within society have to say and when we have to make a potentially life-changing decision. Sometimes we will internalise the way we responded to an incident at any given time – maybe you responded in the same way your mother, your father, your guardian, your teacher, your abuser would have? And you suddenly have to face that you might be turning into a cumulative version of them, something you never thought to be possible? And when it happens and when you have the capacity (if not now, the tools will come soon), face it, deal with it, and add it to your ever-growing archive folder full of moments of learning to be used in the future when that feeling makes its inevitable return to test how you handle it the second, third, maybe even the tenth time around – an older, more mature, eye-rolling adult who didn't really miss life throwing emotional exams at them.

PSA: cheating is not the same as being poly but whatever, that's not what this piece was about.

$\sim$

Kim Windvogel is a poet and writer and works in sexual and reproductive health and rights. They co-direct an organisation called Freedom of Education Motivates Empowerment. They enjoy doing too much and being too hard on themselves. Follow them on Instagram: @blazingnonbinary

Free, So Furiously

A conversation between
Maneo Mohale and Neo Baepi

An inordinate amount of knowledge flows within conversation. So much of my own learning about myself, my ever-shifting identities, and how I view and think about the world has been within chats with other trans and queer people. I've felt myself grow inside from firm yet loving arguments with friends, political awakenings over pillow talk, and firm scoldings from trans and queer elders. Talk continues to shape who I am and who I'm becoming. I think we take talk for granted. Talk is messy, tender, heated, silly, awkward, and filled with contradiction and pause.

So it's no wonder, when I found myself struggling to write about the massively complex topic of 'coming out', I turned to my partner. Here's my attempt to capture a little of that conversation.

MANEO: Okay, kid. Roll call. If we just met, how would you introduce yourself?

NEO: Mmm, Neo Baepi – a photographer. Black, queer and sick of all the bullshit.

MANEO: (*laughs*) Well, I'm Maneo Mohale – a writer, word-worker, tea-lover, nerd. Black, queer non-binary femme. Full of giggles. Okay. The apocryphal 'coming out story' (or stories?). We all have at least one, with all its attendant frustrations, joys, quirks, regrets or surprising moments. Which one is your favourite?

NEO: We had just moved to Cape Town. I asked my dad for us to have a date at Rhodes Memorial. (He had taken a photo of me there when I was like five.) I dunno, I was on some sentimental shit. Nothing to do with Cecil the Evil. Under the guise of testing out my new photography gear, I told him and he responded, 'So does [your brother] have to tell me he's straight now?' I was nineteen, I think. I cried big tears of relief and we never made my sexuality an issue again.

MANEO: I love that story. I know that relief, like a kind of unburdening. I came out to my mom by accident, at the kitchen table, while I was writing an essay about Basotho blankets and their role in marriage ceremonies. The whole essay was basically me musing about how that would work for me should I ever decide to get married. My mom peeked over my shoulder at my laptop, asked what I was writing, and I just blurted out, semi-mindlessly, 'Oh, I'm writing an essay about what getting married would be like for me, since I'm queer.' And she asked, 'What's queer?' I had to close my laptop, filled with so much fear about what I'd just said. That day was filled with lots of tears, talk and confusion. The relief only came later.

NEO: Mmmmm . . . (*hugs*)

MANEO: I think we're both of the position of understanding that coming out, at least in its classic form within popular culture, is something we do for the benefit of straight people. Can we reframe this? Like, what was the moment (or series of moments) where you first 'came out' to yourself?

NEO: I've always liked girls. More importantly, I was perfectly fine with it, particularly when I was a very young primary school child. It only became clear to me that I wasn't always going to be accepted as me throughout my teenage years. I'm okay with us having to qualify things for straight people. Lord knows they can't do a damn thing by themselves. I'm prepared to work with people different from me, provided they are willing to use the knowledge (so freely given to them) for the better. I owe it to my very straight parents for raising a kid who stubbornly loves himself. I would've had a much tougher time as a baby queer if it weren't for them.

MANEO: What're your thoughts on 'coming out' as this kind of 'goal' that queers are implicitly taught to 'achieve'?

NEO: It's easy for 'older' queers to dismiss coming out as something unnecessary, I thought so myself. But when I came out to my dad, it wasn't for him. I knew that he knew. I came out to him because he is important to me, I love him very much and I wanted him and my family to know that its possible to have a queer child who can deliberately exist and own their place in the world. If anything, it should not be qualified as 'coming out', but rather as 'coming home' – to yourself. I think that's important.

MANEO: I really love that. Instead of coming out, we're coming home. But so many don't get to come home, not safely anyways. Safety is always something I think about when thinking about coming out. It complicates so much of what it means to be and exist in the world. Who gets to be safe and who doesn't? How does safety impact the way you navigate, understand and communicate your identities?

NEO: Safety is very important to me. But I'm an insufferable cynic – I know I'll never be safe outside of my home. Instead, I expect the world to hate me and I will always be ready for that. I'm a militant little queer who is ready to fight. I belong here as much as the next upset hetero. I also don't present as straight in any way. If you stay ready, you ain't gotta get ready.

MANEO: I get you. I'm not a cynic at all though (though I do understand how safety is so situational). And also, like we always end up saying, language is so limiting! Being black and multilingual, how do you feel about being able to articulate some of yourself in English and some of yourself in your mother tongues?

NEO: I'm not really able to articulate myself in Setswana when it comes to my queerness. My grandmother has always had me (very obviously gay) as a grandchild. The fact that she'd rather not get to know more about me is unfortunately not my problem. I can't accommodate that kind of violence from my family when I'm fighting real violence from strangers.

MANEO: I felt the schism of language so deeply when I tried to come out to my grandmother in Sesotho. I felt the weight and implications of this language known for it's academicism that we've inherited or adopted from the North and just how incompatible it is with our own centuries-old (and shifting) cultural ideas around gender and sexuality. Like, how do you even say '*Nkgono*, I'm a non-binary demi-gender polyamorous pansexual femme' in Sesotho? Nope.

NEO: (*laughs*)

MANEO: Okay, a cliché (couldn't resist). If you could sit baby Neo down – maybe ten-year-old Neo – and talk to him as you are now, what would you say?

NEO: Challenge everything and everyone. You were born into a body that can do this. Be fearless and happy and free so furiously that they can't ignore you. You belong here.

MANEO: I'd tell Maneo that love is so much bigger than she could ever imagine. And that there's so much of it waiting for her, so many hands to hold her. And the best ones are her own. Okay, so we're far in the future now, magically. In the best possible world you can imagine, what does the world look like for cuties like us?

NEO: Honestly, an ideal world for me is one where all of society effectively minds its own business, from the woman on the train who rudely stares trying to figure out whether you're male or female to the stranger in the public bathroom who won't just let you pee to policies by governments mandated to take care of all its people. There's nothing special about us for being queer and that's the point. We just are.

MANEO: As tough and complex as it is and sometimes gets, I don't ever, ever want us to lose focus on joy. I asked you a little while ago about what gives you hope. What gives you joy now, at this point in your endless journey of discovering and creating who you are?

NEO: At the expense of being very, very corny, I met you. I've always wanted to subvert the narrative that queers are of endless oppression. It's true, we have to deal with a long list of bullshit. But that's not our only story. When I met you and I was given language that would've taken me ages to find myself, that gives me hope. When you build language, you start building a brand new, safer world for people like us.

MANEO: Squee. Thank you, sweet boy. There's so much joy here and so much more to come. So much to be harvested. Next to love, it's the most abundant resource on the planet.

∽

Maneo Mohale is a South African editor, feminist writer and poet. Her work has appeared in various local and international publications, including *Jalada, HOLAAfrica, The Beautiful Project, Prufrock, Mail & Guardian* and *Expound*. She was the 2016 Bitch Media Global Feminism Writing Fellow, where she wrote on various topics, including race, media, queerness and survivorship. She most recently served as the Senior Media Coordinator for Arts and Culture at Collective Media, an up-and-coming media and communications co-operative.

Neo Baepi is a South African photographer and content creator currently living and working in Cape Town. Portraiture is the focus of their photography, allowing them to turn any space into the safest and most intimate. Their work has appeared in various local and international projects and publications, including *The Girl Without a Sound, City Press, Superbalist, OkayAfrica, Mail & Guardian, Common Ground, Cosmopolitan, Marie Claire,* and *Destiny Man*.

The Road to Here

Janine Adams

Matriarchy[8]

noun

- A system of society or government ruled by a woman or women.
  'A matriarchy run by morally superior women.'
- A form of social organisation in which descent and relation-ships are reckoned through the female line.
- The state of being an older, powerful woman in a family or group.
  'She cherished a dream of matriarchy – catered to by grand-children.'

None of those meanings fit what I'm about to share with you. That's ok, fitting in is not something I know how to do.

Mama was my grandmother and she was not from Cape Town. She came here in the sixties and raised her children in this city while her heart was in her hometown, an eighteen-hour bus ride away.

---

8   Lexico.com. 'Matriarchy'. https://www.lexico.com/en/definition/matriarchy. Last accessed 10 June 2019.

I spent so much of my childhood with her. We would make our way to Mossel Bay for long holidays. The trips would take an eternity to nine-year-old me. She always prepared *padkos* for the road, made up of *frikkadels* with egg in the middle, sandwiches, and broken bits of dried fruit and sweets that she bought after pension day from her favourite grocer in the city centre. On the long road east, I would watch the landscape rush by next to me. I always sat by the window until I couldn't keep my eyes open anymore. I would fall asleep on my Mama's lap, waking up to her voice at every little town telling me to use the restroom.

These holidays were amazing times with her and our family. On a typical hot summer's day, my Mama, her bum leg and I took a walk through the kloof. She wanted to show me our old family home. Looking back, it was a kind of pilgrimage for me, learning about my family. She pushed on in utter pain down the one side of this steep hill and then up the other side, leaning heavily on her cane. She never went anywhere without that cane. Catching our breath in the straight, we started approaching a row of abandoned houses. Before I knew it, we were standing in front of the home my mom and so many of her siblings had been born in – a one-roomed shell of orange clay without a roof, no windows, no doors and parts of the sides swept away by the elements and time. What remained was bare, stripped apart. But not for my Mama. We stood there in silence. She was lost in her memories and I was wondering how my grandparents, my mom, and all her sisters and brothers all fit into that tiny home.

She was strict, my grandmother. I remember a few hidings with a wet tablecloth over my tiny exposed legs when I was much younger. She nurtured me with her cooking and her Bible. Christmas time she would make a bowl of trifle just for me. And yes, I still love trifle. Every Sunday, a church elder would come to the house to deliver the blessed sacrament to my Mama. My attendance next to her on the couch was compulsory.

She healed with herbs not with kind words and touch. The emotion she could articulate best was anger, cutting through the person she was addressing with sharpness. 'Thank you' and 'I am sorry' were not her kind of words. Her words were always strong, like her, making me stop dead in my tracks.

Despite her toughness and sense of order, she never once told me 'to act like a girl' or 'stop playing with that, leave it for the boys.' I don't remember her ever telling me what to wear. It just didn't matter. I remember days and days and days with her. Towards the end of her time, we were often alone. She would tell me about things I did not understand. Special things. I would cut her toenails, wash her feet, and scratch her head until she fell asleep. My bed was on the floor below hers and I always felt safe there. I loved and feared her deeply and I miss her still. Now 25 years since her passing, I wonder what her understanding would be of the person I have become?

My mom once told me that when she was pregnant with me, she thought she was carrying a boy. She told a story of going on a carnival ride with me kicking frantically inside her while she was hurling her guts out. This story makes me laugh, even as I am writing it now. I never did ask her what my 'boy' name might have been.

At home, I could wear whatever I liked – shorts and tees on

hot days, and denim and corduroy pants on cold ones. The unsaid rule was that when we went out on religious days and big family events, I would dress like a girl with dresses over my knees, well-brushed hair flowing alongside my face with long, frilly socks and silly white shoes with small holes in the front. I looked ridiculous next to my feminine-presenting younger sister who would be dressed identically. These days were my worst, but I knew better than to wind up my mom. In this way, she is like her own mother and you just shouldn't pick fights you cannot win.

When it came to friends, they were mainly boys. I mean how else could I play with the latest miniature cars, shoot marbles in the sand, catch tadpoles after the rain, and play soccer and cricket in the streets? My mom stopped buying dolls for me early on. My early childhood was free of gender stereotypes at home and when I was with my extended family but unfortunately not on the streets I used to walk. Before I became a teen, I would be called derogatory words referring to a sexual orientation I was not yet aware of. I would not dare take those words home for an explanation, for fear of drawing more attention to myself. It was just not spoken of then.

I remember coming out to my sister during primary school. This was the first time I came out. I professed a crush on a girl who lived a few roads away and who I was becoming friendly with. My sister told me to keep it to myself, and I did.

By the time I started menstruating, shit got real and fast. I was barely dealing with having to wear a training bra! My younger sister, on the other hand, was beside herself. Why was she not wearing a bra and bleeding yet? She was traumatised by not having had these experiences yet. I could not fathom her long-ing next to my angst and confusion. Looking back, while I was wrapped up in all sorts of strangeness about my body, she longed to become a woman, even at that tender age. Many years have passed since the days of me helping her make clothes for her dolls, and we've forged a solid bond of sisterhood and friendship.

*

My mom could not have 'the talk' with me when she picked me up from high school shortly before first break. She said nothing in the car but dropped me at my grandmother's house. Mama gave me some of her herbal tea that she called '*wilde* dagga' and it made me sleep until the late afternoon.

The next day, my mom gave me a book called *What Every Girl Should Know* and more sanitary towels before I left for school. I later asked my classroom teacher to explain what the hell was going on.

Fast-forward to the middle of high school where I am coming out for the second time and to my sister again. This time she cried for me and with me. I don't remember everything she said exactly when I asked, 'Why are you crying?' What I can still feel from that conversation is her love and concern for me. Neither one of us knew what lay ahead, but she knew it was going to get tougher.

My mom and I mostly stayed out of each other's way, while the friends I made at school became my allies. I cut off my pony-tail – the only hairstyle I'd had up until then – shortly after-wards. It was amazing! Meanwhile, my sister and I were learning how to 'Gayle'. This queer slang has its roots in the vibrant coloured drag queen community in District Six during the fifties. For example, instead of saying the word 'beautiful', we say 'beaulah', instead of saying 'coloured', we say 'clora'. The words you want to keep secret are replaced by female names starting with the same letter or, in some instances, cultural or religious references are part of the secret vocabulary. This was our own secret language at home during our teens. We still 'Gayle' now and then when we're talking in front of my sister's children and telling juicy stories, screaming our heads off laughing.

When I was in my matric year, I shaved off all my hair, knowing full well while walking to the barber shop that my mom was going to give me the whipping of my life. It was worth it. The physical freedom I experienced was indescribable. I was changing. I had exited my Christian Union group by then and had experienced a few relationships with older women. I was becoming friends with queer folk while being one of two stand-out lesbians at my school. Shaved pips were banned at school two months later.

That year was rough between my mom and me. There were no manuals showing parents how to raise queer children. Her unspoken, countless sacrifices and her understanding of wanting the best for me did not include this. I, on the other hand, was finding my place and had no other way of being.

Years would pass where my mom and I would be lost to each other. These were strange, cold years filled with darkness, weird encounters and pain. We were all changing – I was pursuing my queer freedom, my sister was starting a family and my mom was healing from her former life. In many ways, we were carving out our own paths.

For most of my twenties and thirties, I was hustling in the food and beverage industry, meeting an array of people, sharing intense realities, cups of coffee, and tempting them with whatever goods were for sale during long-ass days spanning over weekends and holiday times.

In those places I learned how to own my masculine exterior and to accept I'd more than likely stand out in most situations. At first encounter, I know it is my queerness people see first and not that I am a woman. And sometimes, I'm not seen as a woman of colour because of this pale skin I bear. They know I shop in the men's department from top-to-toe. There is no coming out for me.

From that point on, I learned how to navigate spaces by making the people around me comfortable. When I was waiting tables in the nineties, when approaching a table, my attention would be to the male first. By doing this, the straight female would be at ease and the straight male would feel in charge. This worked well because my masculine exterior would then become non-threatening to him. We would share a joke as I worked my 'male privilege' a little and we would be buddies for the moment. It was simple. He was paying the bill most times anyway therefore it was him I had to be in with. Ka-ching.

I learned to master the craft of being inoffensive to customers, always approachable and able to make going the extra mile seem effortless. While to my team, I was one of them slogging away. We spent more time with each other than we did with our families. Once the noughties hit, I was managing establishments and started earning way more than the women double my age who were pushing out the meals in the kitchen. I became the planner, the motivator, the fixer and, sometimes, the whip. My team looked to me for support, guidance, understanding, a gentle ear, and a shoulder to cry on. There was no hiding and all I could be was myself. My exterior was blending with my interior, the harsh with the soft. While friends were having babies, I was nurturing a different kind of family where I worked.

Now, on the streets, it is different too – I am stared at, looked up and down, and I see faces turning away from my gaze quickly. All of them confused or disgusted, I think. You'd think by now every South African knows someone who is queer, right?

I do not care for those eyes anymore and often I do not see them. I am – gratefully – seldom met with physical aggression anymore and no longer walk around with my former fears. My memories of pain are moving further and further away from me. The scars of abuse and violence lie deep within me most days and other days they are a part of my skin or just below it. I am a survivor now, and I learn how to heal every day.

A constant for me are the mild panic attacks when entering public toilets. In fear of being told 'the mens' is next door', and seeing the discomfort my appearance brings to women, especially mothers with young children. The cashier in front of me and the helpdesk assistant on the phone calling me 'sir' do not offend me, as it becomes more embarrassing for them when I correct them. I sometimes laugh at their discomfort and other times I choose not to engage. These are choices I make daily.

Through it all, I am my motherfucken fabulous queer self. A huge part of my work now is training- and development-focused, constantly inspired by strong women all around me. At the office, I am surrounded by my queer tribe and I love it. How can you ever have enough queerness in your day? I live with the love of my life and we have shared almost fifteen years of our lives with each other. You could say we are growing up together. I became besotted with her halfway through my twenties. We were together throughout my thirties and now, in my forties, we are still learning, in love and loving each other so strongly, beyond anything I ever thought possible or dared desire for myself. We host events to create the kind of queer space we feel this city needs – an inclusive, community space, safe for all forms of expression and where everyone is truly welcome.

On the family front, I am accepted as one of many in a long line of fierce, crazy warrior women, while my mom and sister make up my inner circle. We share a love I could not imagine my life without. They are my queens. I am an aunt to beautiful souls and to them I am 'Neen'. Being part of their becoming is an honour and a privilege to me which I hold most sacred. These are blessings not all of us are able to be a part of and share.

And for myself, I am constantly learning to be me, what makes me happy, what to let go of, and what to hold on to for dear life.

⁓

Janine Adams loves life and believes we are shaped by our experiences and driven by our dreams and desires.

Blue Tea and The Beast

Chase Rhys

Trigger warning: suicide

My daddy hits the locked door.

'Be a man! Make fucking open here!'

I can smell the wine through the walls. My heart is beating too fast. My daddy is going to kill me if he gets in here. I can't fit through the small toilet window anymore; my body is too big now. I can't fight my daddy. Everyone in the flats is scared of him. Even the biggest gangsters won't take him on. My daddy don't still worry with guns and panga stuff, he just uses his hands. He's got the biggest fingers in the whole world; they swell out at the tips, like golf balls. Everyone calls him *'Dik Vingers'*. Picking up a straw from the kitchen counter is a real mission for him. I pray every night that my fingers don't start growing like his; my daddy says his hands used to be like everyone else's but when he was my age they started to swell. He didn't mind because it made him the best fighter in the *skeem*, just one *hou* from my daddy then you're out cold. I'm too small now, but one day when I'm big, I'll fight him.

I grab the apple shampoo bottle. My hands are shaking so I struggle to unscrew the *doppie*. If my daddy gets in here, I'll squirt shampoo in his eyes. My mommy slides between my daddy and the door. I can hear her bangles clang.

'Leave him, it was me, I put it on him becau –'

My daddy smacks her. Her body thuds against the door.

I wrap my fingers around the key. My nails stick to my palm; my nail polish hasn't dried yet.

'Mommy?!'

If I open for her then he's gonna get in also. I lay down to look through the crack under the door; my mommy is on her hands and knees, and he's dragging her by her hair.

'Leave her!'

I don't understand fighting; it makes me feel sick in my stomach. I try to swallow but my mouth is dry. I have to get a better weapon than shampoo. I get up from the floor and catch my reflection in the mirror. My face is hot and looks red even through the base. My eyes are huge, I don't know if it's the lash-extending mascara or if it's because I'm *kak bang*. I try to suck the lipstick off of my lips. It just reddens my teeth.

'It's you that's making my child into a *moffie*!' my daddy's voice slurs.

Another smack. It's my fault. I asked my mommy to put make-up on me. I just wanted to look as beautiful and fabulous as she always does. He wasn't meant to come back so early. Now I just want the make-up off. It was a mistake. Kajal and tears streak a black line down my cheek. I look like a monster. I bend over the bath and open the warm water tap. It's so hot it burns my hands but I don't move them away. The geyser makes a noise but it's not loud enough to block out the sound of giant fists punching flesh. I make my hands white with soap and scrub my face. I keep my eyes open. When I close them it feels like my daddy is right behind me. The soap burns but it's a relief to feel pain somewhere on my body and not just inside. I don't dry my face. I look in the mirror – all the make-up didn't come off. It's like my mommy's foundation made my skin waterproof. I scratch at it but the space-shine nail polish leaves glitter on my face.

My mommy is shouting but I can't make out what she is shouting. It sounds like she's speaking with her mouth full of food but I know it's blood. The mirror is getting misty, so I wipe it with my gown's sleeve. Old toothpaste splatters and dust come off but the mirror still looks like it's steaming. It's cloudy; I can barely see my reflection. Is my daddy burning the flat down? I close my mouth and take short sharp breaths through my nose. I don't smell fire and there is no smoke in the bathroom around me.

There's a small thing sparkling on my chest like a hitman's laser from a gun in an action movie. I look down but I don't see the light on my body; it's only shining on the mirror. I touch it and the dot, and it starts to pulse and grow.

Am I hallucinating? Maybe the soap damaged my eyes, I blink hard and look behind me. Everything else in the toilet looks fine. The light in the mirror starts to take the shape of a person's body, a figure hanging upside down. I am definitely losing my mind. The light dims and the body slowly spins the right way up. There, looking out at me in the mirror, is a wrinkled man in a silver robe. Grey dreadlocks are tied in a high *bolla* on top of his head and a single peacock feather sticks out of it. He wears sunglasses with tiny black frames that just covers his eyes. Why does he look so familiar? Wait . . . I hold my breath. When my cousins were here last year, we played Mirror-Mirror in the bath-room and waited for a ghost to appear but nothing happened. Is this the delayed demon? Is this the old man, that Charlie-Charlie ghost that my teachers at school warned us about in assembly?

'Help!'

My mommy's panic sends a cold shiver down my spine. I force all the air out of my lungs, the back of my throat aches and tears tickle the skin around the corners of my eyes. My stomach shakes as I inhale. Why did I have to have so a daddy and why does my mommy always go back to him? You know what, I hope this man in the mirror is Charlie and I hope he takes me away. I'll even go with him to hell, it can't be worse than here.

'Who are you?' I feel ridiculous speaking out loud to myself.

The old man doesn't answer me. He reaches behind him and lifts up a black teapot. It is steaming. He lets go of the handle and the pot floats in the air in front of him. From his breast, he takes out a folded piece of white fabric. With an elegant flick of his wrist, he unravels the shiny silk and holds it over the teapot. The steam licks the cloth and it changes colour; it turns a deep navy blue. He drops the cloth into the teapot. The steam turns blue. I smell sherbet.

My daddy kicks the toilet door so hard the key falls out and slides across the tiles to my feet. The door looks like it's about to give in to his force any minute.

I clench my jaw and turn to the man in the mirror. He's pouring a dark blue liquid from the teapot in to a crystal cup.

'I'm scared,' I tell him.

The man holds his cup out. 'Drink this.'

He has the deepest voice I've ever heard. It vibrates inside of my bones.

I shake my head, 'I don't want to have a tea party now. I have to help my mommy.'

'You have to save yourself first. Only then can you help somebody else.'

It sounds as if my daddy is running at the door and throwing his whole body against it.

'You don't understand, my daddy's gonna murder us!'

The old man smiles, 'Let me kill you.'

'What?!' I knew it. I *mos* said this is Charlie-Charlie coming for my life.

He purses his lips and blows the blue liquid cool in his cup. 'Drink this tea that I made and it will kill everything that you think you are. What you are not, will die.'

What *kak* is this demon talking? He is distracting me. I need to help my mommy. Glass smashes against the toilet door. I imagine my daddy is holding a sharp shard, ready to cut.

'He can't get you if I kill you first. Come drink this.' The man in the mirror takes off his glasses. His eyes are black holes, as if he only has pupils. He brings the cup to his lips and takes a sip. His eyes start to change colour; they shine electric blue.

I shake my head. No way am I swallowing that. 'You want me to drink that concoction and then I'm gonna get possessed and then you can take me to hell?'

'You're already in hell.' He takes another sip. 'This tea will open the doors of heaven for you.'

'And if I'm in heaven then I leave my mommy just so alone

here?' I don't want to die, I have to be here for my mommy. 'She needs me.'

'Drink this and you will save her.'

Maybe this ghost man has powers he can use to help. Maybe he can drag my daddy away in to Mirrorland or wherever he is from. If he wants me to drink his damn tea before he helps me, then I'll do it. 'And now how must I get the cup if you're not even here?

'You must come to me.'

'In there?' I touch the mirror. It feels hot. It burns my skin, and I pull away and suck on my finger tip. The pain is definitely real, so this can't be a dream. Something else is going on here. 'How am I supposed to get to you?'

The man in the mirror smiles. 'You must leave your body and come taste through me.'

'Through you?' This man's riddles make no sense to me. I don't understand. 'How can I leave my body?' I slap my legs and my arms. 'This is me, I am my body.'

The man laughs *lekke* deep from his belly. I bite hard on my bottom lip; I don't like it when people laugh at me.

'Look around you,' he makes a sweeping gesture with his arm, but the tea doesn't spill from his cup. 'Tell me what you see where you are.'

What is this, I spy with my little eye? I sigh and look around the bathroom. 'I see something beginning with a p . . .' I'm too old to be playing this game and now is not the time so I *soema* give the answer also. '. . . a pot-plant.' It's my daddy's favourite thing; he keeps it on the windowsill in the bathroom. It has its own special plant polish for its leaves.

The old man tilts his head sideways. 'And?'

'And?' The shampoo bottle is still open on the toilet seat. 'And Colgate apple shampoo. What is the point of this?'

'Are you a plant or shampoo?'

What type of a question is that? 'No, obviously not.'

'How do you know that you are not shampoo?'

Does this man even know what shampoo is? I get the bottle and hold it up in front of the mirror. 'I'm clearly not this.'

'Why not?'

'I dunno. Because it's just a thing. It isn't alive.'

'And the plant? That's alive – are you that?'

'No, I'm not a plant.'

'How do you know?'

I can hear the cups and plates fall over. My daddy is throwing my mommy's body against the kitchen cupboards. I have to do something to save my mommy but the old man is wasting my time with his silly questions.

'I'm not that *bladdy* plant!'

My voice is loud and angry. I sound just like my daddy now. I don't like that. I wipe my hand across my lips and speak softer. 'I am not anything in this bathroom because I can see it, I can touch it, so it's not me.'

'And your body, can you see that?'

I bring my hands to my face. 'Yes, of course I can.'

'If you watch your body how can it be you?'

As he speaks, I feel like I am levitating.

'Whatever you see, you cannot be . . .'

I feel I'm going higher but my body is standing on the floor.

It's as if only my eyes are rising. I can see the top of my own head – the paths my mommy combed in my hair makes my head look like a tennis ball.

'What is that thing that observes everything, even your own body?' The man lifts his chin as he watches me float upwards. 'You are not only your body. You are something greater. Your body is the weakest part of who you are.' The man gazes at me from the mirror. 'Where are you now?'

My body is on the ground and when I speak, its lips move but I am not in it – I am floating by the ceiling. I watch from above. This is wild but being up here also feels supernatural. 'I am here.' My voice sounds deep and slow, like somebody that's *dik geroek*.

'Do you have a body up there?' he asks.

'No.' I am bodiless but I am still here. I feel light. I fly effortlessly across the ceiling. I recognise this freedom. I laugh the same divine belly laugh like the man in the mirror.

He takes another sip of his tea, and his eyes shine even brighter. 'Are you a boy or a girl?'

'Both . . . and neither. I dunno. How can I say when I don't have a body? I am bigger than gender.' I realise I am speaking in the same confusing way that the man does.

'Last question. Stay up there – answer from the highest perspective. Can you die?'

I answer immediately, 'No.' I look down at my flesh. 'I was here before that body and I know now that I am still here without it.'

'Come here.' He extends his hand out and I am drawn into

the mirror. I move through the glass; it doesn't burn me this time. I am in a cloud, and everything is white. I hover over the man's head. He pulls out the peacock feather from his hair, and his locks come loose. He tilts his head back, looks right at me and says, 'Now!'

Suddenly, I am in his body and watching through his eyes. The cup of tea is in my hands. On the other side of the mirror, I see my body standing in front of the sky-blue paint of our bathroom. I'm still holding on to the shampoo bottle. I sip the blue tea (it's the sweetest thing). I see my body's eyes start to glow electric blue. The old man speaks, 'Now you have tasted the truth – you are not your body. You must use it, live in it, love in it and take care of it, but always remember what you really are. You are the seer. Go live!'

I shoot out of his body and back through the mirror. I am floating in our bathroom. I can hear my mommy crying. If I can go through mirrors without a body, can I also go through walls? I move through the locked toilet door. On the other side, I see my daddy is sitting on top of my mommy. He has a glass of beer in one hand and my mommy's neck in the other. I rush in to my daddy's body as I see through his eyes and I can move as him. I let go of my mommy's neck. She coughs for air. I have to really concentrate on moving my daddy's limbs; he is heavy. I stumble my way to the front door and struggle to unlock it with his *dik vingers*. I walk up the steps to the top storey of the flats. This body is muscular enough to lift itself on to the roof of the *blokke*. Up here, I can see the whole *skeem*. I leave my daddy's body and I sink down through Aunty Mel's flat. She's smoking a cigarette and leaning backwards out her window trying to see what the people on the ground are pointing up at. I move down through her floor and back in to our bathroom. I go back into my body; the return is painless. The man in the mirror is gone. I stare at my own reflection. I'm beautiful, dammit! I hear my mommy's laugh.

I quickly pick up the key from the floor and unlock the toilet. My mommy is limping to the front door. Blood dribbles down her chin dripping maroon splashes where she walks. The room smells like iron. Her eyes are bloodshot and nearly swollen shut but I can see an electric blue shine through. I hear a lot of voices scream outside. I look out through the curtains. The neighbours are standing over something, and they're pointing their phones at something on the ground. I can't see what they're looking at. My mommy walks down the *blokke* stairs, and the people move away when she reaches them. My daddy lays on his back on the concrete. His legs are twisted at a strange angle. Black blood pools in to a perfect circle behind his head like a Catholic halo.

∿

Chase Rhys is a 30-year-old, queer Kaaps author and dramaturg from Ocean View. His debut novel *Kinnes* is the first book to be written entirely in Kaaps and is a setwork book at universities across South Africa. Chase is the winner of the inaugural Adam and Rosalie Small award for best debut writer. Chase is a founding member of the Borderlands Public Arts Project, which is an organisation that uses art and nature to bridge physical and internal divides between segregated communities. Follow him on Instagram: @chase_rhys

Dear First

Ling Sheperd

It comes as no surprise that I am writing to you now. Your absence has been felt and missed, but then I let it go when it became clear there was nothing left to hold on to.

I've been thinking about the many things we said and didn't say. Through all the admonishments and genuine smiles, I thought that I could box it all up, put it on a shelf and say I miss you. But I haven't. I have missed you only.

First loves pass and so do first times, but pulling your heart out of your chest and laying it on a table for someone to keep means you eventually bleed out.

I remember meeting you and how everything was gradual. It was slow and lingering and soft, just like the first time we fucked. I don't even remember if it was day or night or how it happened and why. All I know is the closeness had no time attached to it, no clocks ticking or places to be. It just unravelled and, in that moment, I knew it all made sense. Your big brown eyes were so telling. I'd be remiss to say I don't miss that and how you always smelled of cinnamon in summer and your dad's cologne in winter because he would give you these long hugs before you left home to come see me.

Do you remember when you first told me you loved me? When you first told me you hated me? When you first came back to me because you knew I would be here like I had always been? I am still here. I heard that you came by a few times and, as fate would have it, I wasn't home to see you. What would I have said? If you visited again, would I greet or just lean against something and listen? I don't know if I can honestly say how many times I have imagined this happening, but I do know I always say nothing because I feel nothing, not empty just indifferent.

I broke in half – or told myself I did – when we imploded. We had to implode. It was inevitable. I did not know we'd spend those many birthdays and holidays together. We spent our youth with each other. And I needed you because I wanted you. You came into my life at the right moment as I was accepting myself and also, in the grander scheme of things, my queerness, my otherness, the thing I never had a name for when I was five years old, then sixteen, then 23 with you, and now.

I still can't reconcile having been with you that long only to be shuttled to the side. I got accustomed to being introduced as your friend and to my friends blindly believing I was single for close to a decade. I cried when you said it wouldn't be right if I was a guest at your brother's wedding. I cried when you ushered me out of your home in a hurry without my keys or phone and said it would just be ten minutes, but it turned into waiting at a bus stop for three hours because your friend was coming over and I looked a bit too gay to just be hanging around you. I cried when you said I'm keeping you away from God and you felt you'd lost a connection to the divine that you never had in the first place. I cried when you got the message my sister passed away and never showed up in any way, rather letting your sister-in-law comfort me and sympathise.

I cried too many times in a hapless situation but it wasn't hopeless because there were times I smiled too.

I smiled when you would kiss me awake and say, 'Get up, but let's do nothing and talk.'

I smiled when you rescued me from really shitty friends.

I smiled when you said when I hurt, you hurt.

I smiled when you made an effort to be more open by holding my hand in the daylight.

I smiled when you would only suggest the beach as the sun was setting.

I smiled when you said my space is where you can feel more like yourself.

I smiled when you told me you loved me too much to end it because you were never really loved by anyone and that if I kept looking at you the way I did, I'd always have you.

I smiled and cried over you and with you.

I have a memory vault of lessons and many firsts – like that night we fucked all night in your brother's half-built home. Remember it only had window frames with no glass, a front door but no back one, and you said you couldn't contain yourself when I smiled at you and said, 'What is a home for me without you in it?'

Do you remember that day you asked me to go with you to some abandoned house up the coast because you wanted to fix it up and I was nagging about being out and the sun being too warm and high? I had no idea there was a garden that led to the beach and that you'd hold me in full view of everyone and say, 'I know you ask nothing of me but what I can be and I love you.'

I never failed to love you back but sometimes – not all the time – I think of how I didn't hold on to you enough and that not even the God you say I made you forget could pull you away. Your smell is long gone and I am even beginning to forget what you look like.

You called me queer with such contempt but you are queer too. I never labelled you, it is not my place to. People can be and feel and love however they want. I stood aside as you drifted into another space of self but I never blamed you for it. The absence of self-acceptance is what I blame you for. You saw in me what you couldn't be, what you still can't be.

You taught me that people do place limits on their love and affection towards people like me who live and breathe sentimentality and have unconditional feelings. What is the point of love if it doesn't grow? It should consume in such a way that it is continuous. The connection we had could not be missed and I felt it many times. I felt safe, desired and cared for in the times that you did love me outright.

You have left an indelible mark on me, but it is a stain.

Farewell, my first.
I love you.

Ling Sheperd believes that looking back makes her see ahead. Drink water. Follow her on Twitter: @LingDeeYoh

Mileage

Lester Walbrugh

Morning light has yet to cross our feet. Calluses bump his. I look at mine and hide them under his leg; they need more mileage.

Burnished skin stretches over his length. It contains him, his strength and his every potential. I draw the tip of my finger to his nipple. It hardens. He stirs.

The toilet is hot. It is summer and I have forgotten to leave the window open. A drop of sweat rolls down my back. My pee hits the water in a thick stream.

His embrace awaits me. Morning, says his sleepy smile.

I climb into his arms. They enfold me, like petals.

'How did you sleep?' I always ask.

'Mmmmm,' he always says.

'Last night was good.'

A kiss is his reply.

He runs his nail across my chest and flicks my nipple. It puckers up.

His brow defies wrinkling. His mouth stays set. His eyes dart from side to side, over the whole of mine, and I wonder what he is looking for.

My eyes are calm, an antidote to the fever in his.

He climbs atop. His weight pinches my arm to the bed. I smile.

'I want you,' he says.

'You have all of me,' I say because he is perfect.

~

Lester Walbrugh is from Grabouw in the Western Cape. His short fiction is in Short.Sharp.Stories's *Die Laughing*, Short Story Day Africa's *ID* and *New Contrast* magazine.

This Body Wasn't Always a Wonderland

Sizakele Phohleli

I was thin growing up, as thin as a village girl who fetched water from the river, played rope all day and carried cow dung and firewood on her head every other day. I vaguely remember myself thin, though I never really attached any feeling to it, and never thought it was a feeling that needed particular documentation. Had I known then that these adult days of endlessly feeling ugly and binging on self-hate would follow me, perhaps I would have bottled some highlights where I felt most beautiful solely because of my thinness. But also, beauty wasn't a thing that worried me then. At that age, I was mostly worried about making sure that the blue JoJo water tank was filled to the brim by the time my grandmother came back from pruning all the vegetation in her garden as that meant longer play time even when the night came creeping from underneath our feet, especially in the summer. I was worried about which team would pick me when playing tins or *umgusha* or if I would be an all-saver – a treat I preferred as it meant I played all games without rest, that everyone's victory was my victory, and that my slacks wouldn't be paid much attention.

I remember one specific picture I was in: standing next to

my late stepfather like a lamp while visiting my mother on New Year's Eve in Soweto many years ago. I remember how my mouth formed a shy smile like the opening of a Christmas gift. I remember wearing a Barbie doll dress and a cardigan that was too big and how pointy my knees were next to his tall-as-palm-trees frame. I suppose I was meant to grow into that cardigan. I remember how I held a burning sparkler to his left hand outside our living room door, a village girl with eyes wide open and almost tearing in terror because all this loudness was foreign to me. Why were all these fireworks necessary and, more so, the loudness that they birthed? I stood next to him in awe, never having seen fireworks in my life before.

That's all I remember about my thin days, an awkward bald-headed girl with a shy smile standing next to the only man she's ever called her own – a yellowish-brownish man whose face was fixed in a permanent smile like the Ponte City building in the night whenever he looked at me, like I was a lucky charm from his sherbet packet. This isn't a story about a man who tenderly loved his daughter borrowed from another man all the way to his last bed. This is a story of unbuilding a girl who used sea sand instead of cement to build herself.

Before I knew it, I was the joke of the house. I was the biggest person at home, a testing station for fat jokes that were never funny to begin with but were laughed through with tears in my eyes and a burning coal on my throat. I was always the biggest one in the crowd, the biggest of my friends, the biggest in class, and always mistaken to be older than my older sisters. I hated that I was a sixteen-year-old who looked like three pregnant planets.

I wasn't prepared for this to be honest, from knowing nothing about how I looked to hating everything about how I looked. No one ever prepared me for self-hate but I wore it perfectly.

I had always felt like a flaw. You know that bad taste in your mouth after a heated argument with a lover who's meant to be a soul mate but is not? That's how I felt in this body for many years past my first menses. I have always been the girl who loved every other girl but I wanted to be any girl besides myself. I thought maybe I wouldn't struggle making friends if I was at least pretty and not fat, but I was neither.

I hated myself. Sometimes I still do because even in renewed love for ourselves, our old flaws stay in us and walk side by side with us, their fingers twined into ours without our consent. I am constantly, like a watchtower, trying to turn my old demons into friends. Most days I am friendly and tender with myself, but some days in this body feel like a Monday that never ends. My flaws sound louder and I am more a stranger who intentionally gives you the wrong directions than a lover to myself. I'd been anything and everything to everyone, an oasis to many but always a parched barren land to myself. I offered myself no water and no fruits.

> Remember that time you thought you were dying?
> all the things, all the people you thought you'd never
> live without?
> all the times you thought you were drowning?
> are you not still here,
> not barely but fully alive?

undying?
far from drowning?
even if it feels like you are.
remember everything you've conquered
and let those memories carry you through this fire.
Remember,
you've been here before.

One day, at 28, nothing grand happened. But something in me changed after having walked all the years that matter with self-pity and overflowing self-loathing. I just knew the things I no longer wanted to feel about myself. I was tired of being on top of the list of the things I didn't like, wanted to change, and wanted to get rid of. I was tired of using myself as a whip. I wanted a feeling of belonging to self. Whatever that looked and felt like, I wanted it, as strange a land it would be. I wanted to feel lighter. I no longer wanted to feel like a stuffy house that has neither seen light nor tasted the wind beneath the door and through the windows. I realised how easily I commit to everything and everyone and how I've succeeded in everything I set myself to, but somehow I haven't been able to commit to myself. I wanted to be one of my best achievements even if that just meant no longer looking away from the mirror or switching the lights off when making love to my favourite women. I wanted to be my friend, odd as that sounds for someone who has spent most of her important years hiding from her light. I have loved all my friends with their flaws so why couldn't I learn to love my own?

I wanted to turn myself into a home I'd want my kids to visit during the school holidays should I ever marry the woman of my dreams and start my own family. I wanted to be the beloved face of my daughter's first wire car. I wanted to be the brown, fluffy doll my son wouldn't sleep without. I wanted to look at myself and no longer see faces of strangers I wanted to pray away but strangers I wanted to make nice and play house with. I wanted to know what I would feel like if, after it rained, I took off my shoes when I came into the house so as to not come in with mud, as I did in other people's houses. I wanted to know what it would feel like if I felt for myself the way I felt for others, the way I often made others feel. I needed to become everything I had allowed others to become while unjustly and slowly emptying myself. I needed to become the sum of every love letter I had ever written to a lover, to become both the words and the ink. And it was hard to look into myself with the same affection I gave others.

And so the journey began, and a lot of shedding of old habits became fundamental. All parts of me were required to join the party, even the lazy ones, and all of it was both excruciatingly painful and uncomfortable. New habits had to form, but everything was harder now with all these ambitious weight goals that I still haven't reached three years later. Everything was harder than it was when I was doing nothing but hating myself. This new lifestyle I had to assume was emotionally draining because nothing about me had changed except for my renewed faith in myself. My old flaws were still there with me. My old insecurities still followed me everywhere: into the gym, into the road when running, into healthy restaurants. I became paranoid.

I felt like people were staring at me, whispering to themselves how much I was just wasting my time. I still felt like the biggest girl in the room in every gym class I attended. I felt I ran slower than everyone else because I was so fat, so I started to hate everything. I had set myself up for failure, that was for sure. I cried often. I felt out of place.

The more weight I lost, the uglier I felt, the more critical of myself I became. It was as if the self-loathing had reached a new peak. I didn't understand how sacrificing so much of my favourite foods and devoting so much time to acts that were supposedly meant to heal me would cause so much discontentment within me. I wondered if it was at all worth it? If I had enough strength and patience in me to address my bratty demons by their names? There were many layers that I was never prepared for now that I had finally allowed the old, stubborn light to sit on my lap. What did the new me mean?

Apart from the obvious or not so obvious body changes, it became an endless emotional test. It meant a lot of reluctant no-thank-yous to things I would gladly welcome. It also brought home a lot of loneliness as it meant the loss of friends who preferred me self-pitying and emotionally bare, the friends I had made by laying myself on the cross, drinking vinegar while I fed them grapes. It meant walking away from (not myself this time) anyone who made me feel like I had to run myself down for them to stay or anyone I'd naturally empty myself to fill. It meant understanding that people are not medicine and that no one will ever love me right if I do not love myself right because then where would they learn to love me if not from myself?

It was nobody's fault that I was an endless war, an old recurring war, born from a raging house of a mother – a woman who had as many issues of rejection and whose tongue had mastered all languages of self-loathing just as I have. She unknowingly breastfed us (my siblings and I) the very war her own mother fed her. A beautiful sum of how people could master despising themselves, we'd all – my mother and her offspring – come from dinosaur aches that we wore every time we entered the battlefield. We fought like soldiers who didn't fear death but died anyway. We fought like we were a spreading virus hungry to be seen. I am the youngest of three girls and a few years older than my brother, so you can imagine how many daggers and caskets I'd expertly learned to hold with one hand and one mouth. I'd use myself as bait at times.

It was nobody's fault that I was a crocodile with old stubborn scabs that made staying under water easy. Nobody's fault that I was made from a dragon's lair and a lot of brokenness, so obviously love isn't a thing people from war learn about survival. We learn hate and hate loves us in return. Hate loved me dearly. I'd memorised all the ways I could turn a compliment into a swear word. It was nobody's fault that I was a house of many little fires. Nobody's fault that I didn't give myself due respect, so obviously people only meet you as far and as dirty or neatly as you've met yourself. And I treated myself as a slum so a job well done for those who loved a lover exactly the way the lover loved herself. Whether it was wrong or right, they did to me what I did to myself.

No one took my power, I gave it away willingly.

Move. You are not a tree.

Leave any place that treats your name like a curse.

Your presence may be an insult to them but not to all.

Actively seek those who seek you.

You aren't a house made of paper and paraffin, you are a home to many; your name is a gift to many.

They see your face and all their aches disappear.

Even in the middle of all your flaws, you are the light that lights up their feet in the night-time.

This is yet another painful, necessary lesson.

Leave when you are no longer served the love you deserve.

I wished there was a way I could suddenly be in harmony with myself, with everything and everyone around me without all these necessary growth spurts, weeks of relapses, episodes of breakdowns and losses. I cried a little more at this foreign, lonely land into which I had willingly walked myself. I fell off the wagon for weeks on end and I would get back on whenever. It was a rollercoaster and most times I was failing. I concluded that maybe some bodies were not built for aesthetics but for war, a sword under one-fold, a prayer to survive in the other.

It's okay to fall off the wagon,

the lesson and the reward is not to not fall off the wagon, it is always remembering why you need to stay on the wagon.

keep trying, if you can't do it for yourself please do it for everyone else who depends on your smile for their days to begin, for everyone who holds your name close like a prayer in times of lonely, for everyone who needs you here, alive, more than just gasping for air, breathing freely, I know some nights still haunt you, some faces burn you when you think about them, some names still burn your tongue like hard liquor, I know winter for you never really ends and you are always feeling cold and lonely and colder and even lonelier and you think no one needs you here, you think no one will notice when you are gone, they will, they need you here, you need you here so keep swimming even if it feels like something is pulling you down, keep trying.

do it for all the times you didn't give up, for all the times you pulled through for yourself when everything within you told you not to, do it for all the times you loved yourself through all your lonely, through all your pain, this here that hurts you right now cannot be the end of you.

don't give up.

please don't give up.

In this journey, I have since realised that the size of my body was never the main issue. I've had many hidden issues within me since childhood and my weight was just a loud, ringing church bell resounding every thing I still needed to do within myself. I used my body as an overstuffed scarecrow because I needed something to help me keep away from dealing with my own rottenness.

Finding, or rather returning to, oneself isn't as clear-cut as people think. It is hard and it requires a lot of cleansing, a lot of starting anew, a lot of shedding of people, of your old self. Getting your head right about yourself is tricky. How strange that it is so easy to love anything and anyone outside of you. One morning you have spent many days in the sun loving yourself wildly and passionately but the following morning you feel engulfed by so much darkness and self-loathing and you don't know how to go forth and what to do to shake this feeling of unwantedness off. Like a recovering drug addict, but in my case the drugs have always been other women. One minute I'm mastering all the laws of staying away from where I am not wanted, and the next drunk night I am back on her texts, begging her to give me one walk in the sun.

I had to – and still have to – keep reminding myself that I am literally the most beautiful woman I know. This version I am currently manifesting is my best work yet. I have known no other house for as long as I have known the body I am in.

There's a kind of happy only you can give to yourself.

Strive for that happy.

Pray for that happy because that happy requires a lot of self and self isn't always pretty, self is sometimes ugly but always worth the while.

When you do find it, after many times of peeling yourself like an orange into yourself again, after many nights of choking on your own tears, scrubbing the dirt off of you, hold on to that happy as if your life depends on it.

Pick that happy over anything, over anyone, but this kind of happy doesn't come easy, it will cost you everything you were once sure of, it will cost you a lot of people, it will reveal many enemies you've confused for friends, friends who have loved you bent but could never bend for you, this happy requires you to forever be present, it requires you to tirelessly show up for yourself, it means recognising that on most days you are a shitty person, it means acknowledging that at times you are a fault and owning up to those faults without bitterness, without reducing yourself to only those faults because there's more to you than all your mistakes combined, there's more right about you than there has been wrong. This kind of happy means you are forever shedding people off of you, dressing yourself up in a lot of prayers because to meet such night parts of yourself, you need faith, you need a God who isn't human, who stays with you despite your many nights.

This kind of happy means you are constantly protective of your space, endlessly standing up for yourself in spaces that previously preferred and loved you for your silence, this kind of happy means deliberately leaving any place that doesn't soothe your soul so most times this kind of happy brings home a lot of necessary lonely and this lonely doesn't taste like honeycomb and Christmas biscuits, this kind of lonely cannot be fixed by disappearing, or drowning yourself in things, in people who have mastered taking from you without you even noticing, it requires you to be painfully present, even on days you would like to remain dead for an entire day.

but pray for this happy, and choose this happy over anything, over anyone.

Three years later, a novice marathon runner and healthier in all the ways I think about myself, I look at myself in awe and I wonder if perhaps this is what the sun and moon look like when meeting at Orion's Belt? I'm still an old ruin who now waters herself more than she sets herself ablaze. It took me almost three decades in this skin and this body to learn that in the end, I am my best lover.

In this quest to redefine myself and to wiggle myself off of my inherited self-hate, I learned I am endlessly walking through the darkness. Everything I do I have never done before and is, therefore, new. I hope that my little light will lead me to more light – a light that requires even more light. It's a necessary obsession that should never end.

I have learned so much about the process of being, of pacing oneself with kindness, and the mathematics of coming undone gracefully in your own hands. I have learned to embrace each day as it comes. Some days are worse than others but some days are good, really good, and on those days my feet feel light on the ground. Nothing is pulling me in. I am deliberate, wide awake and my laughter is no longer a cry for help. On these success days where the sun finally rises in me, I am aware of everything I am feeling. I document every single feeling, every ounce of light I let in and the darkness I keep out. I document the colour of everyone's smile around me and the voices of those cheering me on because I will need them later. I actively remember what I am wearing, remember what the day smells like, and count out loud the spoons of brown sugar I let melt into my coffee because on these days the shower water tastes like water and not my tears. My dreadlocks don't feel like ropes around my neck so that when the worst days come – they will definitely come – and make me feel like a prisoner in my own skin, I remember the happiness and victories I am capable of. I remember why I stayed in this dream for so long and why I cannot afford to jump ship. What I know now is that sadness is no longer my place of comfort as nothing ever grows there.

stay here.

be present.

you are exactly where you need to be,

it may not be summer where you are right now and the sunflow-
ers may not be blooming a million summers yet, we can't go
through all nights sleeping, some nights require us wearing our
eyes wide open and far from dead, some nights are made fully of
rains and loneliness, necessary rains, a necessary lonely, but you
need to be here, fully present, even if it burns many parts of you
leading you to your glory, stay here, wide awake, this is how fire is
made.

~

Sizakele Phohleli is a boy's name. She was named after a nurse who
helped her mother give birth. She is her mother's third daughter after
twins who are as beautiful as the rising sun. She has a brother four years
younger than her. She is happy here. She is happy now. She will persistently
be happy tomorrow. Follow her on Instagram: @her_mentality

Coming Out: A Series of
Strange Events
Tiffany Kagure Mugo

Coming out is weird.

The whole concept of it is a little squiffy to say the least. How does it make any sense that someone has to come and say, 'Hi, I have been doing some thinking and feeling and having one crisis after another and have realised that I do not want to love and fuck the way the world tells me to.'? The whole idea of coming out is a dual-edged sword. On the one hand, it is an important political statement, a way of ensuring that the space you are in does not bring about any nasty surprises because some homophobe is lurking in the shadows. There is something powerful about being able to own a part of your identity in a public space and tell the world they can shove it. On the other hand, there is something somewhat unnecessary and even a little degrading about it. Why must I come out as if my sexuality is the equivalent of confessing I'm about to take explosive substances onto a flight or smuggling contraband? 'No need to be alarmed people. I am just carrying 1000 cc of alternative sexuality here.'

There is a lot of pressure on the certain idea of what coming out should look like which causes me to wonder about the nature of coming out. Why must it be a declaration and not an existence? Why is it that it is seldom seen as coming out unless there is some big announcement? I cannot recall a single conversation in which I sat anyone down, handed them a warm cup of tea, looked them squarely in the face and said, 'I would let both a man and a woman see me naked.' I have never gone and told someone that 'I may not end up marrying a man and not because I want to end up jetting around the world with my pugs in a purse but because I could end up with a woman.'

Wait, that is a lie. I once emailed my mother telling her that 'I have had two girlfriends in the last three years', but that is a story about The Great Twitter Outing of 2012. To be precise, my coming out was a series of actions rather than statements – some of my own doing, some thrust upon me, some that just casually wandered by with a quick nod and a 'How you doing?' My coming out mirrors how I have come to see my sexuality in general: a series of messy and unrelated events and pieces which, like life, sometimes have no rhyme or reason. They are, like all facets of myself, simply . . . there. No more or no less than the things that surround them but all the while adding to the strange tapestry that is my existence. My coming-outs sometimes tumbled out of my life, sometimes were pushed, sometimes were placed carefully before the world. Some coming-outs were far more significant than others but all adding to the ever-growing tapestry that is my (messy) rainbow quilt. Life is wild and made up of a series of tales, so let me explain my continuing journey into my sexuality with a few of my own. They may seem random and out there but isn't that what it is like to 'come out' – a series of strange (sometimes stand-alone) stories? Here are mine:

Hide and Seek and Secret Kisses

The first time I kissed another girl I was six. It was around that time at least – I just know I was super young – that age where hide and seek was a serious game. It happened then and it always happened when we were playing hide and seek. Always during play dates with a family friend's twins who I hung out with by virtue of our caregivers always hanging out together. The more dominant twin would always make her sister be the seeker and we would hide. Fast forward twenty plus years and I sometimes see the twins on Instagram and wonder if they remember. I know they are queer, but do they remember that it all kicked off when we were so young and innocent – without the 'influence of media' and deep in Kenyan society's family Sunday Funday?

Funnily enough, it was my first – but not last – foray with twins. I have had three sets in total, five separate people if we are to be exact, but that is a piece for another time. This was just the first in a series of experiments with girls while I was in school, which all culminated in a threesome in matric with two of my friends whilst a third watched. We were all experimenting and would quietly and calmly pack those memories away afterwards, but it was those twins who started the cobbled path.

The Great Twitter Outing of 2012 and The Great Facebook Exit of 2014

The year 2014 was a big one on social media for me. Social media will pull you out of your closet like a pack of wild horses. When we first joined Facebook, some of us used it for our close circles, family and close friends. The more the networks grew the more we forgot about the people hiding in the shadows. Facebook algorithms were kind to me, and lurker family members, like the aunt who posts too many religious messages and the uncle who still doesn't get how to upload a decent profile picture, fell even further into the shadows.

Then I started HOLAAfrica and splashed all its sex-positive, bubbly queerness all over my timeline with reckless abandon. HOLAAfrica is the wine-fuelled brainchild of myself, my partner and our friend, and is a digital hub dealing with sex and sexuality. We just needed to see queer women on the internet from Africa but there was nothing. So we decided that there should be a blog and that grew into a whole social media network, publications, workshops on safe sex and pleasure, manuals, podcasts and general sex-positive, digital wildness.

Cue the rumours and whispers. They swirled all around me and when they eventually came to a head, I freaked out and started a 'gay Facebook account' for myself. It quickly got shut down as 'not being the account of a real person'. Facebook basically said that my concentrated queer self was not my real self. A space where I shut out a whole bunch of people and would not let them in was not who I was anyway. Looking back at the posts and what I did on that account, I realised that Facebook's misguided policy, although a potential harm to many queer folks out there, was right in this case. I was not being a real person by having an account that *only* looked at the fact that I now saw women naked on a regular basis and liked it a lot. So, after muttering 'Well played, Facebook', I went back to my old account with a caveat status that read: 'This profile is going to have a lot of things that may shock you. Some of you were blocked and are now not blocked. Welcome to the Thunderdome.'

After a while of article posts such as *How to Eat Pussy Like a Champ* and *Ten Reasons a Straight Woman Must Not Say She is About to Go Gay*, I realised long statuses were the bane of my existence and Twitter was a much better place to go and be messy. This is how I was subsequently outed to my mother on Twitter – she inherited access to my account when she decided my old phone was now her new phone. Valentine's Day mentions of how my partner was my Valentine's date led to many questions and even more tears. As well as the aforementioned I-have-been-dating-this-woman-for-two-years email. Just like that, social media had me out of my digital closet.

Baby's First Relationship

There is nothing that will make you question everything about yourself as a warm-blooded, sexual, emotional being quite like your first girlfriend. They will come into your life and tip over everything. This was no different for me. The genesis of the journey towards truly engaging with my sexuality came as one half of a confusing twin package. It took me a while to legitimately tell them apart, partly because we were long-distance and partly because they really did look so much alike. And dressed alike. This was the least confusing part of this relationship. During this time, I also casually announced to my friends that I had hooked up with a woman and what made it most interesting was the confusing situation that framed the entire announcement.

It started on a friend's 'last weekend' of freedom, as she was about to embark on what she claimed was the last relationship she was ever going to be in. It involved her lover, her lover's twin sister, too much drinking, a politics test I had to study for, a somewhat aggressive offer of drunken sex, my housemate screaming 'Just fuck her already' from the room next door, and a sheepish apology as they made their way back to the wild from whence they came, aka Johannesburg. The next thing you know, I'm in a relationship with a woman from Botswana whose taller basketball-playing sister warns that she 'will hurt me if I hurt her'. This relationship lasted eleven months and was the first true grappling with my sexuality.

Not only was there the whole holy-cow-I-keep-seeing-another-vagina-every-time-I-have-sex reaction to contend with but there was also the back and forth in terms of religion, friendships, social circles and navigating a love life that was contained to rooms and whispers and secrets. My life at the time was trying to figure out: did I even like this girl? Were the fights worth it? What did it mean to be gay and go to church on Sundays and be the shy little queer in the back listening to people speaking men into their lives? My friends thought it was cute now but there were questions of 'when was I going back to men?' All this was wrapped in a vortex of the most emotionally draining cycle I had ever found myself in. There were constant fights and make ups and 4 am calls when I had a class at 8 am. It was a mess. Throughout all this, not only was I coming out to friends and all those around me (mostly because I used to sob a lot in class because of yet another fight with my girlfriend) but also to myself in a lot of ways because questions of 'Is this what I want? Is this who I am?' would constantly move through my brain as I continued with the relationship. My first girlfriend was the living embodiment of the existential crisis that grips most people when it comes to dealing with their sexuality. That's probably why those relationships are quite often a shitshow and it is a lucky few who escape the monumental mess of a story that is dating another woman for the first time.

An Academic Exercise in Being Gay

In my academic life, I used these short steps to be in the academic space for long periods of time. If you choose to follow them, repeat the steps necessary to you:

1. Choose a topic loosely connected to my experiences, preferably something vague around women.
2. Get a girlfriend.
3. Completely freak out about having a girlfriend and being a Christian.
4. Change thesis topic to *An Examination of the Relationship Between Religiosity and Homophobia in Uganda.*
5. Get a first-class pass.
6. Continue to freak out about religion and being queer.
7. Have a monumental break up.
8. Swear off women.
9. Find the love of your life and start a queer womanist platform.
10. Write a shit ton of academic papers about WSW (women who have sex with women) and sexual practices.

'Is Tiffy a queer? What is a queer?'

So what are the family members saying on WhatsApp now that everyone has a family WhatsApp group? In our case, it is usually used for memes, religious messages and to tell everyone that they are late for whatever family event everyone is invariably late for in Naivasha because, truth be told, Naivasha is far. It is also used to send articles about me and my work in queer archiving and activism with the accompanying message: 'Someone wrote about Tiff's work on the internet'. In true Mugo family fashion, the fact that I am called a queer activist is not brought up despite the fact that everyone low-key knows what queer means, either the problematic version or the new woke version. Do I make a big hoopla about it? No. Are they whispering about this? Yes. Is this a formula that I have chosen to copy and paste in other scenarios such as bringing my androgynous girlfriend wearing a bow tie and male dress shoes to a family wedding? Yes.

There is an element of privilege on my part to be able to manoeuvre like this. Firstly, I have always been the wild one – the one with the big personality and the one who is a little bit left of centre with her ideas. I have always been the colourful sheep of the family and just an oddball in general. This has allowed me certain graces such as my aunts only trying once to hook up my perpetually single self before never trying again and also never being asked where my boyfriend is. This has grown even more since I became 'the feminist one'; people dare not poke the bear. Secondly, the weight of my work successes has allowed me a generous amount of wiggle room in terms of what I am allowed to do. I write about sex. A lot. Much to the heartbreak of my ever-suffering mother. But the thing is, my writing about sex and running HOLAAfrica, despite being outside of the norm, has led me to have a career with all the right markers. Cash flow: check. Articles in prestigious spaces family actually reads: check. TED Talk: check. Jet-setting home for two days then flying out again as was the custom for my grandmother who was our very brilliant matriarch: check. To quote a problematic movie: the kids are alright.

In this vortex of happenings, there are the ever-present clues that I am not straight. No declarations, just breadcrumbs that will lead down the right path. Take it at your own risk. For me, coming out was a series of things happening, a series of things that continue to happen. Outside of these, huge events have been a series of normal days, holding hands with my girlfriend, tweeting about our joint Netflix account, and bringing up a queer perspective in a conversation after a few glasses of wine by prefacing almost every statement with 'You straights are really bringing us down, fam.' As recently as a few months ago, I came out to a new friend and classmate who kept calling my partner 'he'. And I won't lie, it took me a long time to correct her. A lot longer than, now that I think about it, I am admittedly comfortable with. Even though you can literally Google how queer I am, it is one of the best kept secrets in my life.

The thing about coming out is it never really stops, it is more of a marathon than a sprint. As long as we live in a world where being heterosexual is seen as the norm, there will always be one more room, one more classmate, one more workplace, one more new friend, one more crush, one more family member that you have to tell, 'Hey! I am a big flaming queer person and I eat rainbows for breakfast and as a light afternoon snack.' This is exhausting and causes me to wonder if it is worth it.

Granted, there is a power to owning your sexuality in spaces, especially as a queer womxn in Africa no less. But sometimes there is a great power to simply moving through the world in a way that speaks to your entire truth in all its random messiness. Sometimes the idea that one has to come out initially perpetuates the notion that this particular identity must and should trump all others and be presented as above and beyond all other ones. If this is part of your politics, then this should be something you do, but the idea that you must always present your sexuality can also be problematic because it can be something one has to declare to warn others. Coming out is as much about what you do and who you are as it is about what you say, but what you do can be wide, different and ever-changing.

∽

Tiffany Kagure Mugo is the intoxicatingly scary gatekeeper of HOLAAfrica, a Pan-African, queer womanist digital community dealing with sex and sexuality. She is a TED speaker and bad-ass board member of the FRIDA fund, as well as a writer, media consultant and freelance journalist who tackles sex, politics and other less interesting topics. Once upon a time she was an Open Society Youth Fellow and now has dreams of studying some new things. During weekends she is a wine bar philosopher and polymath for no pay. Follow her on Twitter @tiffmugo and on Instagram @kagsmugo.

Journey of a Lifetime

Gulam Petersen

Sometimes they give me money just for talking. This is what people don't realise about sex work. Sex work is not only about having sex, about penis and vagina. Sometimes clients just want to talk about their lives, about things they can't speak to other people about. We provide a service just like the milkman used to deliver the milk. I deliver a service.

I was born in Worcester, Riverview, to a coloured mother and a black Xhosa father. As far as I was concerned, my upbringing was like any other child's in the small community of the Boland. Growing up, we were four children. My father passed away when I was five years old. My family members would openly tell my mother that there was something wrong with me, but she always told me that there was nothing wrong with who I was. People at school started calling me a *moffie*. They called me *moffie* because I liked to play with so-called girls' stuff like dolls. I loved dressing them up and giving them makeovers too. I enjoyed cooking and the first pot of food that I cooked was a coloured staple: *koolkos* (cabbage food). My younger sister taught me how to do needlework after she learned how to do it in high school and I loved it. I knew from my early childhood years that my sexuality was different from most of the other kids, although to me my feelings felt normal. Others, especially my extended family members, constantly tried to tell me it was wrong to be who I was and, since I was still young, they would say to my mother, 'How can your child know anything about sexuality and gender identity at this age?'

I left Worcester as a young teenager, around the age of thirteen. When I came to Cape Town, I went to live in Tafelsig in Mitchells Plain, and I also finished high school there. The location is predominantly coloured and I had to face a lot of stigma for being a *moffie*. The people called me names and the bullies all lived in the community. Luckily, I had three friends who embraced me – Edwin, Theodore and Jerome. We became close friends and they allowed me to explore my identity: I would make them snacks, I would make them coffee, I would dress how I liked, and they made me feel safe. Later, I had affairs with all three of them! They didn't know about each other, of course. I think it was just their time to explore their sexualities too.

The first time I came out openly was when I returned to Worcester for a weekend to be confirmed by the church. My family all belonged to the Old Apostolic church. I was sixteen at the time and I was dressed in a white blazer suit. My pants looked like bell-bottoms and I wore a cropped jacket with a lacy top. On that day, the words that came from my mother's mouth were heart-wrenchingly beautiful. In front of my whole conservative family and church members, she said, 'Baby, my child, you are becoming a young adult. It's time for you to stand, pick up the pieces and carry your own cross.' She went on to claim me as hers as she stood in front of the people who continuously gave me a hard time for living my life the way I saw fit.

My mother never had any issue calling me by my preferred gender pronoun. She told me, 'One thing that will never change is that I brought you into this world and I will stand and support you in any way that I can.' She said that although people call me a *moffie*, she was the one who birthed me and she carried the pain of labour. Nothing that any family member or church member could say would change her mind. She will not reject me to please family, society, community or whoever we live around. I am her child and, until the day she closes her eyes and dies, nobody will prove otherwise. I cannot explain to you how this made me feel to hear my mother say this after all these years, after all this time. It felt like winning the Lotto and not being sure what to do with your body in that moment. It was surreal.

I was introduced to sex work 30 years ago. I was nineteen and I loved it! When I leave home at night, there is a concern for my personal safety. When I get ready to leave, I say a prayer to be and to feel safe because a lot of trans sex workers do not make it back home. Many of us do not return home because our clients 'discover' that we are trans and sometimes we are killed or beaten or simply disappear.

When I enter a new client's car, I always wonder if he knows that I am trans or whether it would be a 'discovery'. In these moments, a lot goes through my mind because if this client doesn't know and 'discovers' me, it could lead to me not returning home. We face a lot of dangers as trans sex workers, even our own sisters mock us on the street because they do not want us to have clients.

Even when clients tell me that they know that I am trans, it still bothers me. The last time someone said this to me, I was punched and beaten within an inch of my life. If it weren't for two security guards who came to my aid, I don't even want to know what might have happened.

All sex workers face dangers unbeknownst to the public due to sex work still being criminalised. People see us as objects to use and abuse as they please, and they forget we only strive to survive and put food on our tables and to buy a new, sexy outfit sometimes because we cannot look the same every night. I wonder if people realise how important it is for sex work to be decriminalised.

Wake up people! Wake up government! The time is now to set all sex workers free – freedom from being treated like a criminal. We need everyone's support because our lives matter. I matter.

$\sim$

Gulam Petersen is a trans sex worker and a happy feminist. Call her Gulam by day, Lady Regina by night.

They Called Me *Stabane*

Andiswa Mkosi

I think the funniest story I have heard my family tell about me over and over again is the one where I, as a toddler, continuously rejected the idea of wearing a dress. Growing up, I lived with all my cousins and aunts in our grandparents home Gugulethu. The friends I made there were mostly boys, and when we played our favourite game, *Poppiehuis,* the kids would naturally delegate and then assume gender roles. Because I was born 'a girl' they would force me to assume the role of the mother. Oftentimes, I would get super-pissed and intentionally isolate myself from them and the game that was supposed to be fun. This feeling of being mis-understood greatly affected my confidence during my formative years. I would purposefully alter parts of myself to accommodate people and situations around me in order to fit within the commu-nity and our greater society. I think as kids, we like to challenge one another. My sexuality was challenged by peers – in such instances like when we were playing *Poppiehuis* – way before I got to naturally give myself over to internalise my own understanding and exploration of my own sexual identity and long before I even knew what the word was, or meant for that matter.

When these games were played, remarks like *'uyintombazana*

into oyiyoAndiswa, yiba nguMama mfondini' meaning, 'You're a girl Andiswa, you must play the mother role,' were always called out. The translation sounds really fancy, but the force and anger with which it was often shouted at me stung hard, painfully and sat with me always. And so this was my childhood life, often having to defend how I dressed, what my preference was, and having to face the fact that no one ever allowed me to be me besides my mother and immediate family.

The minute I stepped out of the house, my life became an internal and external warzone. People would loudly proclaim their shock at my dress code. Shopkeepers would look me twice over, never sure whether to refer to me as a girl or a boy – my existence confused the hell out of people. When I look back on it now, I can laugh about it, but isn't that what we do? Laugh at our trauma in order to heal and move along. If only I knew my power back then. If I knew my power, maybe it would have been fun to play along with those people. If I knew my power, I would have enjoyed watching them sit in their discomfort while they tried to figure out my sexuality.

When I reached primary school, things started to get a little more interesting. I guess you could call it: Level Two – Andiswa figuring out their identity. My primary school was in a predominantly 'coloured area' and, with a segregated history like South Africa's, that's just a whole other essay on its own. Gugulethu, a predominantly black community, and Manenberg, a predominantly coloured community, are separated only by a highway, although they are both part of the Cape Flats. I crossed this highway for the first time when I started primary school. A lot of the learners who schooled and lived in the Manenberg and Surrey Estate areas would question why we, as black people, were coming in to their areas and their schools. Interactions were hostile and difficult to navigate. Excessive quarrels and fights would frequently break out. I was the 'Khoza girl who keeps herself like a boy'. Fighting for my identity, place and gender was a constant in my life, no matter where I found myself.

It was here that I met a girl who became my friend, but the weird thing about this friendship was that I always felt nervous around her. I would go out of my way to make sure I impressed her. When kids would say something against her, I would fight them in order to defend her, but it was only in high school when I started engaging in conversations about same-sex relationships, interacting, and seeing other people who identified as queers that I understood that the primary school girl was my first crush and that I was romantically interested in her all that time. Maybe if I was taught that these feelings are valid and deserve to be explored, I would have interrogated my identity from a younger age. Up until this day, I go to social media to check up on my first girl crush to see how they are doing in life.

Looking back, my years of growing up in Gugulethu, coupled with the years of primary school in Manenberg, really formed the foundations of what was to come later in my life. Truth be told I was, and remain, one of the lucky ones. Because I started to attend an all-girls high school, I had access to people who were having interesting conversations about their sexual and gender identities and how they chose to express those identities – the type of conversations I really needed to understand who I was and who I wanted to be: the Andiswa and Andy Mkosi people know me as today. My idea of queerness is constantly evolving; I am still learning about my own queerness and that of the people around me and I am honoured to have the opportunity and access to never stop exploring and evolving.

$\sim$

Andiswa 'Andy' Mkosi makes music for herself, a black queer woman, simultaneously delivering a critical view of modern life with a deep exploration of self. Her body of work collects stories, tells of wet dreams and women crushes and holds contemporary society up to the light to see where the holes are. In 2016, she launched *The Bedroom Tour*, a series of live music performances in the homes of her fans. Follow her on Twitter and Instagram: @AndyMkosi.

Breaking Down the Walls: Colonial Legacies, Home and Heteronormativity

Jamil F Khan

When asked about my views on social justice, I have very little in the way of optimism and excitement to offer. Reading, writing and doing social justice is exhausting and sometimes dangerous. I am always only one degree of separation away from the fate of my slain ancestors whose only chance of surviving, with their humanity intact, was resistance. It is a resistance that has come to distinguish the air we breathe in this fraudulent republic currently known as South Africa.

Privilege and, by implication, oppression are built into every institution we currently subscribe to. Inequality is the premise on which 'civilisation' is built, and every brick of every building we now parade as markers of achievement bears its legacy. For these reasons, when Helen Zille makes those repugnant statements calling the legacy of colonialism into partial acclaim, she digs into the gaping wounds many of us carry. The legacy of colonialism is always only negative when each of its supposed benefits still evades many of us, including me. The truth goes much further than piped water and ornate architecture.

This story is a reminder that for many queer youth, home is not a place that is easily found, if it is found at all, behind the walls of 'normal'. To many, buildings and the uses we find for them are arbitrary. But to me, the buildings I have inhabited throughout my life have enabled my sometimes comfortable discord with heteronormativity while identifying as homosexual. I anticipate that there will be many family resemblances between other experiences of oppression and mine – I strongly encourage connecting the dots, especially in relation to my point about the enduring exclusion colonialism has created. Here, I engage with the work of various theorists on the constructs of gender, sexuality, family, effect and power to weave a personal narrative describing life as a queer person in a heteronormative world.

The Forming Years (Cape Town, 1989–2012)

The home that I knew for 21 years of my life took shape in a house situated on the outskirts of Cape Town. It was the first home my father had financed as 'our own'. Placed in a middle-class coloured suburb, our home (which was considerably more embellished than others) became a symbol of ultimate desire, not only for my parents and me but also for our neighbours. Growing up, this was mostly what I was surrounded by: heterosexual, married couples with children, pets, gardens, paved driveways, garages and backyards. These living arrangements were hailed as the ultimate symbol of respectable living. Important to note here is that for many coloured people, the restrictions placed on them by the apartheid state predetermined what they could achieve and, for many, this kind of life was a sure vestige of proximity to respectability, more specifically white respectability. This was all I saw around me despite my niggling intuition that my homosexuality was a boarded gate to this respectability. Subtly, I began to co-opt myself into being less homosexual because the risk of not attaining the ultimate standard of respectability proved more dangerous than choosing something else. Bordieu states that the dominant definition of the normal family rests on a 'constellation of words – house, home, household, maison, maisonée'[9] which seem to describe social reality but actually constructs it. The home consists of related individuals who live under the same roof. It is safe to assume that this nuclear family unit is a heteronormative one which decrees a particular hierarchy. In my experience, this certainly held true in my home and many others; my father was the sole breadwinner while my mother was the homemaker and nurturer.

This was my first induction into the 'heterosexual matrix'.[10] Judith Butler describes this matrix as 'that grid of cultural intelligibility through which bodies, genders and desires are naturalised'. This is premised on 'a stable sex expressed through stable gender [. . .] that is oppositionally and hierarchically defined through the practice of heterosexuality.' Taking into consideration these interrelated concepts of home and heterosexuality, I remember experiencing emotions of despair and fear for my obvious inability to achieve this. I would not be able to enjoy the economic fruits symbolised by the free-standing house in a neighbourhood filled with heterosexual, nuclear family units who epitomise wor-

---

9   Bourdieu, P. 1996. On the family as a realized category. *Theory, Culture & Society,* 13(3): 19–26. https://doi.org/10.1177/026327696013003002

10 Butler, J. 1990. *Gender Trouble: Feminism and the Subversion of Identity.* Routledge: New York.

thiness and respectability. I remember constantly going back and forth between admitting and denying my sexuality to myself in an attempt to convince myself that I still had a chance of living my discordant sexuality undetected if I just performed it properly. Being queer in a world that sold me the opposite was characterised by anxiety and shame. The constant threat of wrath for transgressing was all around me through subtle reinforcement, which taught me to regulate myself in grand Foucauldian style.

The people around me who consciously or unconsciously partook in this project of disciplining my sexuality practised their power through discourse. In no particular order, I remember my mother, brother and sister-in-law all promoting normalising discourses peppered with varying degrees of objection ranging from disapproval to disgust. While watching an episode of *Oprah* with my mother one afternoon at home, she commented on the subject of parents dealing with their gay children. In response to the show's encouragement of acceptance, she said, 'This is fine, as long as they are not my children.' I remember realising that despite how close we were, she would be my first opponent if I were to choose an authentic life of fully expressing my sexuality. She proved me right when I eventually expressed it. When I was twelve, my brother once remarked a sentiment of disgust in relation to gay people with the word '*sies*'. A warm rush of blood punctuated my face as I realised that I am a phobogenic object[11] to him without him knowing. Here again, shame surfaced. He still finds me hard to accept, if only for the fact that I am not

---

11   Fanon, F. 1956. *Black Skin, White Masks*. Pluto-Press: London.

approved of by his beliefs of what constitutes a 'normal' life. My then sister-in-law reminded me that I am transgressing a standard when she asked me when I am getting a girlfriend. The normative assumptions made by the 'when' in her statement implied the inevitability of heterosexuality which I knew would evade me. Listening to all of this generated feelings of imprisonment. The symbolic violence of this discourse locked me into self-regulating retreat for fear of punishment associated with transgression.[12]

The power that these processes had to co-opt me into being a docile, normative subject was overwhelming. I remember living in the future, anticipating the consequences of confessing my supposed deviance. Confession often seemed too dangerous and I could imagine only three possible outcomes: live in perpetual unhappiness married to a woman, declare myself asexual (based on a narrow understanding of sex and sexuality at the time), or commit suicide. While still trapped within the confines of dependency, every day was an unsuccessful assimilation attempt to become as unexpressive as possible to escape the dissection of the normalising gaze on me. I remember here, more than anywhere, is where I adopted a peculiarly muddled habitus. Unpacking Bordieu, Ashall states that 'habitus refers to those dispositions that "generate practices, perceptions and attitudes that are not consciously co-ordinated or governed by rules, but nonetheless are regular enough to appear consistent."'[13] Because I was not

---

12 Foucault, M. 1978. *The History of Sexuality* (1st American ed). Pantheon Books: New York.

13 Ashall, W. 2004. Masculine domination: Investing in gender? *Studies in Social and Political Thought*, 9: 21–39.

comfortable, my affective and gendered habitus[14] often did not correlate, which created even more anxiety in me about what was visible enough to expose my discordant sexuality. Simply put, I was constantly anxious that my gender expression would alert people to my sexuality and I would be shamed for it.

Eventually, I used confession to come to truth. The consequences were not what I had imagined, but this may be because through confession, I appeased one of the most central notions in the workings of power – submission. I would, however, like to think that I challenged the power my parents had to construct me after confessing my sexuality by stating that they should not make it about themselves but remember that it is my truth to bear. I also resisted the discourses of deviance by reminding them that I was the same person they had known; they only had new knowledge of me as of that moment. This theme of confession would replicate itself throughout my life for years to come, without me realising that it is an effect of a power that constrains me.[15] The fact that I felt I had anything to confess proves that, despite my resistance, I was still subject to the power of a discourse that constructed me as deviant. The ultimate 'not me' figure, as Garland-Thomson puts it.[16]

14 Adkins, L. & Skeggs, B. (Eds.). 2004. *Feminism after Bourdieu*. Blackwell Publishing, Malden: Oxford, UK.

15 Foucault, M. 1978. *The History of Sexuality* (1st American ed). Pantheon Books: New York.

16 Garland-Thomson, R. 1997. *Extraordinary Bodies: Figuring Physical Disability in American Culture and Literature*. Columbia University Press: New York.

The House of Dreams (Gauteng, 2012–2015)

I moved to Gauteng in 2012 to live with a close relative and her family. I was welcomed in a state of fresh revolt against the rules of my parents' home. I was ready to become my own person with preconceived notions of success and individual merit. The house we lived in was built from the ground up – a highly significant event for the family as this made for an obvious success story. It became the template for my own definitions of success. I recall how the house was always lit up at night. This served to reinforce the tangibility of their success so that not even darkness could erase it for a night. There I learned to model myself after and aspire to something that remains unattainable to this day.

Living there was raw materialism. Capitalist heaven. I was groomed for personal success at the expense of my sexual identity. Capital in all forms including economic, cultural and social was the most important commodity. The conversion of capital into its various forms was a daily strategy.[17] Feelings of longing and desire characterised the everyday for me, while trudging a daily routine of chasing wealth and happiness. The idea was sold to me that I too could achieve all of that if I was willing to become less like myself and more like my family. This meant becoming more hetero-sexual, masculine, inconspicuous and less emotional, intellectual and sensitive. The affective economy[18] of my life was best described as suppression.

---

17 Bourdieu, P. 1986. The forms of capital. In J. Richardson (Ed.) *Handbook of Theory and Research for the Sociology of Education* p. 241-258. Greenwood: New York.

18 Ahmed, S. 2004. Affective economies. *Social Text*, 22(2): 117–139.

The suppression was fuelled by the policing tactics of my new-found nuclear family unit. The lines of self and other were clearly demarcated by my relative who constantly policed the length of my hair and the style of my clothing. Anything that resembled a performativity[19] which read as feminine was decried, while anything that read as masculine was applauded. So I learned the rules of engagement in this world of material lust. Again, governmentality kicked in as I succumbed to the disciplinary bio-power wielded over me, for fear of being denied the means to achieve success.[20]

Her husband rather unintelligently used gender to police me and my body. As a means to reinscribe ideas of my inferiority in relation to him, he would always deconstruct my sexuality to mean being female-like. This discourse is not only imbued with notions of inferiority but also of being a space invader.[21] He would always comment on how having me around was like having two wives – clearly a mark of transgression in a monogamous, heterosexual utopia. The transgression was my tolerated presence: a male body marked with feminine gestures and attributes. I presented a threat to the fragile notion of stable masculinity but at the same time presented a perfect candidate on which to practise patriarchal domination outside of the realm of deplorable gender inequality.[22]

19 Butler, J. 1990. *Gender Trouble: Feminism and the Subversion of identity.* Routledge: New York.

20 Foucault, M. 1977. *Discipline and Punish: The Birth of the Prison.* Vintage Books: New York.

21 Puwar, N. 2004. *Space Invaders: Race, Gender and Bodies Out of Place.* Oxford: New York.

22 Foucault, M. 1978. *The History of Sexuality* (1st American ed). Pantheon Books: New York.

Domination therefore perfectly describes the politics of this period in my life. The power exercised over me as someone in need of mercy kept me constantly subordinate. I was in a constant state of apology because my very being was transgressive. Like the pursuit of happiness through material things, the pursuit of normativity proved to be a futile project. I never achieved it. The more I modelled myself on my family, the more I failed because they were also modelling themselves on something else and so the rules kept changing. It is this symbolic violence of chasing a dream that could never be achieved that carried on into the next phase of my life, on different terms.

'Let's play house. I'll be the Mommy!' (Centurion, 2015–2016)

When I moved into my own apartment in May 2015, I believed I had left behind all the policing power structures I'd endured under my family's roof. I later learned that these systems have an insidious nature with far-reaching arms. This time, it was the model of heteronormativity that replicated itself in my newfound home. Living with my boyfriend at the time, I seemed comfortable within the very system I problematised as discordant above. Here, the project of attaining heterosexual, middle-class respectability continued. I was renting an apartment in a security village, had financed a car and started making a home. The materiality of being proved messy. I was the sole breadwinner, while my boyfriend was unemployed. Yet because I presented as more feminine and he as more masculine, I found myself taking on the traditionally female gender role of nurturer.[23] A constant balancing act involving my own need to assert my power as a breadwinner and his fragile male pride ensued. Implicated in the heterosexual matrix once again, I experienced emotions of frustration, duty, confusion, overwhelm and, eventually, indifference.

Discourses around domesticity flourished in this space for some reason. It seemed to encourage the replication of heteronormativity in this and another same-sex relationship. An obsession with domestic chores as a gateway to cleanliness and therefore respectability manifested in my partner who would always insist on cleaning things. It seemed at times to be a slight at my refusal to engage the banality of domestic life but also a yearning to recreate a familiar structure of the heteronormativity he grew up with. It was not the striving to cleanliness I look at as heteronormative but the pattern of domestic labour that requires division of labour prescribed by traditional gender roles.

After this relationship ended, a second relationship continued the trend. This partner once said, 'If you did not know how to cook, we would not have a relationship. I am a man after all.' The implication that cooking was a prerequisite for a relationship with him, superimposed with the move to privilege his masculinity as salient over mine, took heteronormativity to a new level of absurdity. However absurd, I was proud to have performed my feminine gender role to pass this test – comfortably discordant. This experience later led me to develop an aversion to domestic

23 Butler, J. 1990. *Gender trouble: feminism and the subversion of identity.* Routledge. New York.

chores for a while.

The power that these blatant and subtle discourses had to induct me into submission still astounds me to this day. I, as a gay man who comfortably performs femininity, felt it my place to remain submissive and obedient to the egos of the men I was dating. I conducted myself in accordance with roles and positions that constructed them as masculine in relation to me. Again, self-regulation manifested. No matter how frustrated I was by this, I had made psychic investments[24] in the role of the 'good wife' like the one I saw my mother play. It gave me pleasure to know that I could do all of that as a man. It provided me with another outfit to try on. After the end of my second relationship, I realised that I had been wearing someone else's clothes. I experience darkness when reflecting on that time of my life – a perfect metaphor for the consequences of gender as we currently know it.

Home is Everywhere (Johannesburg, 2016–2018)

In 2016, I decided to stop chasing happiness as it had been sold to me in the form of cars and houses and exclusivity. I stopped everything I was doing to decide what I wanted. I gave up my job, sold all my furniture and moved to a new apartment in the Maboneng Precinct in Johannesburg CBD. I stopped living a life that had been scripted for me by regulating my preferences and desires. I had my entire life wrapped up and handed to me with instructions to follow. I rejected all the subjectivities imposed on

---

24 Coleman, J. S. 1990. *Foundations of social theory*. Belknap Press of Harvard University Press. Cambridge.

me[25] in pursuit of something unfamiliar, yet decided on by me alone. My resistance was choosing, in some cases deliberately, the polar opposite of all that I'd aspired to before. I realise now that I am still engaged in a happiness project of some sort, imbued with symbolic representations of unattainable ideals. The difference now is that it is a project of my choosing and not one that I have been co-opted into.

Where I stand now, I do not attach value to any one particular ideal over another. I particularly do not aspire to achieving respectability through the symbolism of spatial and geographic positions. I believe I have little power to transform the discourses that previously shaped my being but, in my act of resistance, have chosen not to engage them. They therefore exist outside of me now. I have not yet come into being anew, nor do I think that process will ever conclude. It is an ongoing process of negotiation and redefinition. In order for me to live in a state of ongoing emancipation, I will be resisting imposed subjectivities for the rest of my life. I will change my mind countless times and slip in and out of subjectivities that suit and strangle me.

This is the fluidity of identity[26] I have struggled to acknowledge before. It is now my project to be as varied and inconsistent as I choose to be, if I choose to be. I am by my very construction, the antithesis of stability and a threat to the monolithic categories of identity a male-dominated, heteronormative, het-

25 Foucault, M. 1982. *The Archaeology of Knowledge.* Pantheon Books: New York.
26 Onorato, R. S. & Turner, J. C. 2004. Fluidity in the self-concept: The shift from personal to social identity. *European Journal of Social Psychology,* 34(3): 257–278.

erosexist world tries to construct. I no longer have an interest in engaging my being in ways that are not informed by my choices. The city, and the way downtown Johannesburg tends to be a bit chaotic and messy, situated the building where I lived in the context of its relation to the many surrounding buildings. I choose this as a metaphor for a different way of relating to the world. I am constantly in exchange with the people around me, and through this I experience a constant flow of subjectivity. I see it as something to be exchanged, redefined, deconstructed, renegotiated and decompartmentalised. All the while, I stand at the helm of this process wielding agency. I, as a subject, may never come into fully being, but I can come in and out of being.

Reflecting Forward

I look back on this journey with pride and immense sadness. My pride is something I contend with and remain critical of lest I be fooled into thinking that my individual choices have liberated us from the systems that inspired my resistance in the first place. My sadness, however, is motivated by feelings of grave loss. What many take for granted has taken so much from queer people. I was reminded of this pain by writer and critical diversity scholar Zanta Nkumane with his article *Daily Moments of Loneliness*.[27] Nkumane reminds us that queer experiences are marked by feelings of unfulfillment: many black queer bodies carry a virulent unfulfillment, which I can't trace to a particular source but can

---

27 Nkumane, Z. 2018. Daily moments of loneliness, *Mail & Guardian*, https:// mg.co.za/article/2018-10-12-00-daily-moments-of-loneliness. Last accessed 5 June 2019.

only suggest that it bears the stains of children who never got to be whole. The unfulfillment of teenagers who never experienced a full, open teenage love affair and adults who still fear holding their partner's hand in public. Even if we don't experience rejection by our families, we enter into a hostile society that has us in a perpetual state of 'holding back'. I experienced Nkumane's entry into a hostile society the day I was born. From the hospital to my childhood home, I have been housed in buildings that were created in service to heterosexuality. Being denied participation in the full, open teenage love affair Nkumane speaks about brings me back to the realisation that the structure of the 'neighbourhood' as discussed earlier prohibits homosexual desire and withholds protection for queer innocence. So we find ourselves adrift in a sea of unfulfillment, further battered by the violence of heteronormativity gushing from the walls of every home we enter, in hopes of taking refuge from the other afflictions that attach themselves to us.

I am compelled to bring this into awareness in relation to the legacy of colonialism which lives to enjoy reverence in the imaginations of some. Far from idealising pre-colonial society, my understanding considers that the idea of 'house' and 'home' is currently predicated on a structure of European invention which remains at odds with the humanity it claims to protect. The legacy of colonialism is always only negative when viewed through an intersectional lens because infrastructure and architecture are always first imbued with meanings that exclude people in physical and symbolic ways. When we do not all have access to the protective structures colonialism built due to the systems it invented and colluded with, there are no positive outcomes for anyone, especially the children who never got to be whole.

Amidst calls to constantly move on from the past, work remains to be done in bringing the long arm of that past into awareness. If today, I am still reminded of the limits of my own existence in a world I can still recognise as prohibitive, I fear that progress will keep slipping through our fingers as foundations cannot be built on weak and shifting sands.

~

Jamil F Khan is a writer and researcher currently enrolled for a PhD in Critical Diversity Studies at the University of the Witwatersrand. His research focuses on the histories and lived experiences of creolised people (classified as coloured) in South Africa and more broadly explores power dynamics between oppressed groups in a white supremacist world order. He considers his work to be a bridge between academic and artistic spaces to give expression to the historic tradition of storytelling which is too often trivialised and dismissed. He is currently writing a socio-political memoir due for release in 2019. Follow him on Twitter and Instagram: @ JamilFarouk.

Love Thy Neighbour

Nicole Adele Adams

Trigger warning: rape, abuse and mental health

I will never forget the first time I made sweet love to a woman. It happened on my birthday, 20 October, but don't ask me to remember the year. I remember this day because my mother baked a cake for me – a dark, deep and delicious chocolate cake. She baked it and proceeded to slap me in the face with it. To this day, I still love chocolate cake. I don't know how I can love something that one of my multiple abusers made for me. Yes, my mother abused me, but she wasn't the only one.

Later that evening after the cake debacle, my neighbour, who was my crush and had witnessed everything, came over with her own version of a birthday present. The first version was a chocolate muffin she had also baked for me. Then we shifted our bodies under my bed, our favourite hiding place, and she kissed me. I closed my eyes and we made sweet love after we ate her perfectly baked muffin.

Now my neighbour might have been my lover, but I was already in a relationship with someone called Bianca. Bianca went to another school – she was white and all the boys wanted her, but *she* wanted *me*. My neighbour was always jealous of Bianca. Personally, I loved all of the attention, but I think I truly loved my neighbour because when I didn't see her I was deeply unhappy.

As a kid, I shared a room with my two siblings and we slept on bunk beds. At night my stepdad would enter our room and he would have his way with my body while my siblings were there. I still hope they didn't realise what was happening back then. Whenever he raped me, I would close my eyes and build a wall to deal with my trauma. I think that now, as a sex worker, I am happy to take men as clients because I still build that wall when I am with male clients. I do not want to be with a man when I go home. I want to be with a woman because that's where I can take down my walls. I come from a lot of trauma. My stepdad was not the only person to rape me. We would be pawned out to strange or familiar men and three of my four kids are fathered by blood relatives. My twin sister died at the age of eight due to rape and my stepdad was in the room when she was raped and when she died. My doctors call me schizophrenic, but I wouldn't say this is true. I believe what they call schizophrenia is my twin sister still living inside of me.

My youngest child is the product of gang rape. Initially, they couldn't do the rape kit properly because I was in a coma from the incident. They finally performed the rape kit when I woke up from the coma and two weeks later, as I was leaving the hospital, they told me I was pregnant. I was informed that I had the option to terminate the pregnancy, but I decided to continue with it. Today, my baby is one year old and she is a mini-me. She has my cheeks and she is beautiful.

I have never raised any of my kids, but I want to be a mother to them and I am still looking for the meaning of family. I want to be a part of their lives, but I must focus on myself and work on who I am first. I think it's important for people to know that the abuse I endured – emotionally and physically – has nothing to do with my sexual orientation. I am a Christian. I am who I am, and no one can tell me that being a Christian means that I cannot be a sex worker and a mother, that I cannot be queer or that I cannot make decisions for my own life.

~

Nicole Adele Adams is a fun-loving, exciting and outgoing person who loves learning new things and exploring. She is a mother of four, a sex worker, a proud queer, a poet, and believes that you should always read the contract before you sign it.

Radical Softness as a Weapon for Liberation

Qondiswa James

Prologue: November

There is a picture in my head. Curled-edges, bleached of much of the colour. At the centre of this picture there is a moment untumbling into itself. The beginning of time there. The slow coming of things, making themselves pictures, stars, dust. An amorphous, liquid thing that swells and crests with no sharp edges. Time beginning there. I think I see the first breath being taken, lifting things to live. I watch the cosmos on the water unfold DNA becoming matter, growing wide and leafy. Green now. The crawling things, the walking things, the roaming things. Time begins. Man walks upright and finds himself here. I am born in the Transkei on 6 November 1993 on a dusty patch of the N2. On the way to the hospital, I claw my way out of my mother's womb. I think I am excited and impatient; rocking in my mother's belly, I had heard the siren call of the living and I am greedy for experience. My mother lies on the back seat of the car and screams from the side of the road; my grandmother is the midwife. I don't know where my father is, maybe in the front seat looking out or maybe kicking stones a little stretch away – an attempt to stay out of what he has been taught does not concern him. He looks out at the neat yards of rural homes, at the green rondavels and orange houses, at the men *esibayeni* (by the livestock enclosure) hovering around cigarettes

171

and slow conversation. Women from nearby villages stand peering wor-
riedly behind fences at the edge of their yards. They have been labouring
under the Eastern Cape sun turning the earth a deep, fertile brown that
will gift crops before the next winter comes. Every now and again a truck
ambles past with a long, low hoot of greeting or encouragement, a car
rushes forward. Between mother and grandmother I am pushed out,
purple and bloodied in afterbirth, gasping and crying. By the time I turn
25 I have experienced a most profound heartbreak. I recognise the
brooding brow of a black man and fall into the long-forgotten familiari-
ty of Daughter, somewhere between little girl-child and seductress. 'You
tricked me,' I will say by the time it is over, gasping and crying, intes-
tines hanging around my neck. 'And there in the trickery I fell.' My
father, dead now, reaches out to me through the seam of memory and
I feel the haunting severity of patriarchal authority and answer to it. He
is born almost ten years before in a hospital in Khayelitsha. By the time
I am in boarding school – a tender four-year-old who doesn't understand anything but feels intuitively that something is not right with the
world – he has joined the PAC. By the time I am in a private boarding
school, trading homesickness with rich white kids whose only life am-
bition is to inherit, he is an anarchist. No longer cradled in genesis, I
fall in love with the ghost of my father, and I do not know how to move.
Kubi. (It is devastating.)

May

'You're asking me if you can cheat and calling it freedom –
what's wrong with you?'

It is May, autumn, and she asks for her freedom; her lover does
not understand.

'Monogamy is counter-liberation,' she tries to explain herself. 'Lately, I have begun to believe that monogamy is the legitimising frame of heteronormative capitalism. I accept that maybe in today's system the best chance of survival is behind a white picket fence, but I don't think the human animal is inherently monogamous. At some point, from stardust and gills, we become human. We stand upright and go to hunt and gather. I don't think at that point we're overly concerned with soul mates and white dresses for wedding days, a dog, a cat and two-point-four kids. The monogamous nuclear family is a recent invention, capitalism's trick to hitch the survival of the species to itself for its own survival. It performs ideological functions for capitalism: the family acts as a unit of consumption and teaches passive acceptance of hierarchy. Marriage is just a systemic logic to help keep tabs on who's behaving and incentivise them.'

For the first time, her lover looks at her as if she is something foreign, something strange and suspicious. She continues with feeling, 'Do you know that spouses don't pay estate tax? That medical aid, disability, and veterans' benefits can be transferred to spouses? That trusts can only be done between married people? Hetero-capitalism rewards monogamy and ostracises the anomalies. If I let the system think for me, I will give myself up for some ideal sold to me on celluloid of the perfect thin, blonde white girl being kissed at "I do". Miss me with that bullshit.'

Her lover stands at the doorway of her bedroom, the walls a clean and white container. She is collapsed at the bottom of her lover's bed, crying and pleading, and says to her, 'We're both pretty smart. We can figure this out.'

Her lover's brow is pained and furrowed – but she will not cry tonight. 'No, we can't.'

It goes on like this. Years of a relationship wept out and drained in four hours or less. She is clinging to the memories of her lover's face in sleep, the slow, soft blinking of eyelashes seemingly looking at her, and how clean everything always is, white and pristine. Her lover's hair is sleep-fuzzed and redder than ever in the pinkish hue of her bedside lamp; she is exhausted. It is 1 am and she answers in short, clipped phrases, her breath enough only for the rhythmic pumping of pain through the blood. They are at an ideological impasse. At the end of it there is no more touching, just the gaping wound between them.

'I will scrub myself of myself until I am clean enough for you, worthy of you.'

She knows her lover will not wait.

November

There is another moment, similar to this one. I sit on the red brick stairs of the outside garden. My friend Goitsi is next to me. We are wearing similarly pink clothes – she in loose pants flowing a darker pink, and me in a salmon skirt. It has been warm for the past few days in Cape Town. The air is still, sticky, clouds hanging low. It is always dusk. Without the pink, it is dust clogging the air of blue, drilling down with the city's building machines. The city is ablaze with dust and dusk. We sit smoking a spliff. There is a palm tree in the garden that hangs over our heads, its leafy green canopy always dappling sunlight for shaded afternoons. We breathe like this together.

'I've been thinking about yesterday's chat,' Goitsi says. 'Radical softness.'

I 'mmmm' and murmur in agreement. It drops into me: radical softness. We'd theorised it yesterday under the same condition, this our cycle of lunchtime hooky to smoke cheeky spliffs under this breathing, green palm tree, at our feet a hundred more green things: weeds, roots, flowers, food.

'I will be brave in my ethical self. As I quest for liberation, I demand integrity to go with my serving of justice. As I strip myself, now understanding there is no purpose but to be here and choose it, I strip myself to first find on this physical body – chained here to this carcass on this land mass still breathing – how the human might be. From this body. How might the knuckled rings of the metal noose be unloosed from this body? Dreams spread out at my feet, I have laid here on you and breathed with you. Deliberately. I show the crisscrossing stitches and scabs and marks stretching landscapes on this, my body. I do this deliberately. I say to you, "I am undressing now; I am trying to be more human with you." I do this striptease of wounded flesh for the fire in your belly. I say to you, "Look what it is for this body clawing at the cliffs edge, nails scrabbling at useless holds of earth to cling to freedom. I want to see you. I want to be seen (by you)." I do this dance of vulnerability under the hooded gaze of your bedroom lamp. I am naked before you and real. Nothing but pink, all inside-mush pink. Salmon-like tongue forced around carcass, like I am flayed or pulled inside out. I ooze, lush and wet, and simperingly whisper, hoarse throat unsure, asking you, "I'm scared. Am I safe here?" Your arms circle and surround and you lie to me, yes. And I, on a different land-scape curling into a wet, hollow Petri dish spilling out, I yes, I open. Brave and sad, I pick at old scabs and show you where it bleeds sometimes. Radically soft.'

Goitsi lifts her glasses and folds them on the red brick stairs. Her purple lips smile and purse and pout, speaking, 'I want to be this radically soft. Radical and soft. Sad and brave. Soft oozing wound, healing. I think I can be. I think it is not too much to ask.' She pauses, 'I believe in God,' she says. 'Her and I have a difficult relationship. I've stood at the abyss and wondered at the wounds, the wounding, the wounded. But that is not what God is for. God's not finna meddle.'

I think of an old movie. The story goes that at first there were the gods. But then the gods were bored, so they invented humans. But they were still bored, so they invented love. Then they weren't bored anymore. And then they invented laughter, so they could stand it.

June

It is June and she has fallen in love again. She asks him who he is seeing and he tells her that he is polyamorous and she exhales. Here, she hopes, there exists the possibility of an ethical way to love with the wholeness of herself. He is an anarchist and a fem-inist, a cishet who fucks like a lesbian. He is taller than her, with dimpled cheeks and bright eyes. He has the most blinding smile she thinks she has ever seen; he is so beautiful to her. Not equipped to pick apart the actions of the patriarch and separate his intentions, she falls.

She makes it clear, 'My heart is soft and open and my spirit is willing and thin with it, homie. Please be kind to me.'

'Okay,' he says.

She kisses him under the shy eyes of streetlamps glaring from their dark edges. She has been living with her white housemate for four months now. Fresh black graduate anxious for a roof in the suburbs of Cape Town, she had asked her white friends to finesse their connections. In February she had been introduced to her new housemate by their mutual friend and she finds fresh ground to root. Theirs is a two-bedroom flat in Mowbray, in their lounge, two fading blue couches and a fireplace. They live on a corner street close to Main Road with its Pan-African spill of hairdressers, tailors, electronics shops and internet cafes. Outside, there are the tired grumblings of Golden Arrow buses and the incessant drone of 'Mowbray/*Kaap*' from *gaatjies* in the windows of passing taxis. There is a mosque with green minarets down the road and in the early evenings, she sits in the garden and smokes to the mournful tenor's call to prayer. Sometimes she catches the high-pitched laughter of schoolgirls snacking on Spookies and the hushed transactions of the local dealers soliciting their supper.

'I'm going to ask you three questions and then probably make a statement.'

He looks at her from the sides of his eyes, 'Okay . . .'

'You don't have to answer.'

'I know.'

The first time they make love, it is underwhelming and inevitable. He sits stiff on the fading, blue couch in the lounge, hands folded on his lap, peering past his eyelashes at the pot plants, the books, the Buddhas.

'*Zezakho ezizinto?*' ('Are these things yours?')

She is in the shower with the door open listening to the music filtering in to the room, the steam pregnant with sound and potential.

'What would I be doing with *izinto ezinje? Noba ndihlala nomlungu, soze ndide ndibenguye.*' ('What would I be doing with things like this? Just because I live with a white person doesn't mean I'm going to turn into one.')

'Oh,' he says, 'okay.'

She, wrapped in a towel half-wet, water still drying on the tips of her unshaved legs and pubic hair and dreadlocks, asks if he would like something to drink. Something to smoke? Tea? Yes, she has tea, and puts on the kettle, feeling sensual with her hair down and heavy on her shoulders. He doesn't like jazz but listens without comment. At this juncture, he does not know what he is doing. He has been pulled by her nature, her tendency to glitter and simmer in dark places. He has no forethought, no plans, only feels the tugging of something sharp from inside himself. He knows there is something about sex here between them – if only because she has told him quite clearly, 'I want you.' She had said this on a bright blue day, a sheen of sweat on their faces, the rush of traffic in front of them as they stood on Main Road.

She had asked him three questions and to his credit he'd only lied about one. Or obfuscated. Or omitted. The last few women he was with had set his car on fire. Four women who'd banded together for purposes of justice torched his tyres in broad daylight, holding up placards of demonstration: *INJA MAYITSHE*. (THE DOG MUST BURN.) ONE PATRIARCH, ONE BULLET.

He has not told her this story yet as she lowers herself in a loose pink dress on him. He is still sitting on the couch, now and again clutching the hot mug of rooibos without sugar and without milk. Like she drinks it. But she is having wine tonight. She is smoothing her sharp edges to play the role of heterosexual – somewhere between little girl-child and seductress. She looks at him also from batting eyelashes and presses her chest to his. She exhales into his pelvis with hers, 'Um . . . do you wanna . . . I don't know, I don't want you to feel any typa –'

'*Ja*, let's go.' He says this sharply and abruptly.

He has come here for this, this sex between them. Has come to crawl under the naked knowing of another woman. He hears too often of who he has hurt. He cares and still cannot resist the siren call to crawl under the naked knowing of new flesh. Mostly, he is not thinking too much about it. Later she will accuse him of violence. But not yet. For now, they take off clothes under the stars on the wall of her bedroom (a gift from her ex-lover), and she giggles at this new body now naked on her loving bed. She, unbeknownst to him, has also come to crawl under the naked knowing of new flesh. She has come to learn something. For her education, she comes to appreciate the following things about him: he is black, he is political, he is from the township.

'*Ndiyamonqena lo mlungu wakho*,' ('I'm uncomfortable with this white person of yours,') he says to her the third time they are intimate. 'Small talk with white people in the suburbs isn't really my thing. *Nchono ndik'se eKhayelitsha qha wena.* (Better for me to just take you to Khayelitsha.)' He is an appropriate whip for her self-flagellation. She sees herself through his context and he tells her, 'Yes, you are white.'

And she beats herself for class redemption, desperate to bleed out her middle-classness. He, smiling and dismissive, a grown-up boy with big feet, clumsy-like actions without intention.

September

I feel still with you, grounded. I sleep curled, pressed tightly against your back. You shift. Restless, we turn and toss. Our legs and feet are tangled, your hand squashed between your chest and my back, which I would like you to kiss sometimes. I press my mouth against your shirt, make an imprint of lips and a whisper of cotton. I slip the material up, make an imprint of lips and whisper that I love you. I so worry that you will go away from me. We wake up and I tell you, 'I am in love with you.' I want to tell you I feel still with you, grounded. Sleeping restlessly, I had slipped my hand over your waist and up your chest between your forearms and felt you press my hand into you. I do not know if you love me, but this is enough.

August

It is August, Women's Month. She is sitting on a panel that he has organised to reflect on ways forward in the wake of #Total-Shutdown and she says something stupid like, 'Middle-classness does not exist.'

After, he drives her home in silence, parks, and asks what she means by this. He is patient with her through her unlearning, gentle and resolute. Of course the middle class exists.

'You are trying to commit class suicide,' he says to her.

She does not disagree. 'I worry I will always be operating from fundamentally flawed politics because of what I am, an accident of birth that put me in private school and replaced my mother's tongue with the Queen's. I wonder sometimes if I should just be doing the work with the so-called middle classes.' She is scared that she has fucked everything up. Heart in palm, she holds her breath and asks him, 'Are you done with me now?'

'Why?' he is gentle and resolute. 'We're building.' He is lying but this will come out much later. For now, she misconstrues the personal and the political and he lets her.

On Saturdays she finishes work and goes to the station to catch a taxi to Khayelitsha. There is always at least one person in the taxi with their heads hanging heavy between their knees, their friends having bundled them up in to a corner to nurse their drunkenness on their way back to their mother's house. At night, the taxi rank at the Cape Town station dissolves into something like a street party. It is loud and full and drunk with feeling. It smells of stale urine and braai meat. We drive on the N2 past Pinelands, Langa, Gugulethu, Crossroads, Driftsands, and on to Mew Way, where the M32 turns a corner to the place where black people are always dying, curious outsiders bumper to bumper to lay witness to wreckage. Inside, the taxi smells of breathing humans in too-close quarters, but this is a familiar thing here. Sometimes he is already by the Site C rank to meet her. There is a brightly lit Caltex garage not too far away and he instructs her to get off there and wait for him. The taxi drivers speak loudly to each from their bellies and their hooters, big bodies of metal around them congested on the narrow street, swerving the deep puddles of potholes gravelled through tar and concrete. Other times, he is not there yet and she stands in the shadows between two containers, hiding from the hands of men reaching crook-edly for intimacy. She waits for him from her corner in the dark. Often, while she waits, he is watching an Orlando Pirates soccer match. She shouldn't, but she likes this about him, the simplicity of his particular masculinity. They talk about a lot of things. Or she talks and, in between Orlando Pirates soccer matches, she genuinely believes he is listening to her. They are lying in his bed. The door is open to the darkness of the living room beyond. In it, there is a deep red carpet and black leather couches facing a disconnected TV that has been long out of use. He is messy like her – weeks of unwashed dishes stacked haphazardly in a pink washing basin. She has taken off her shoes outside the door to his room. His linen is striped and his bed is unmade, and from the window she sees the neighbours' rooftops and the streetlamps coming on as the daylight fades. They speak quietly to each other.

He says to her, 'I have always been poor.' Says it like it is his, like it is the something that he knows for sure. She envies him this clarity of place. He is a man; he is an anarchist; he is poor. He wears the last like a defence. Later, her friends will laugh and call it a smokescreen for pathological misogyny and she will not disagree. But now, clothed in her cloak of middle-classness, he feels so distant to her. Those like her. They have always been so foreign to him, though he has had many of them, as foreign as white women with strands of blonde hair like wheatfields on his pillowcase. She tells him that she sees him and he is beautiful to her. She tells him that she feels safe and he tells her there is nothing wrong with that.

She asks him, 'What is polyamory?'

And he says to her, 'Free love, anarchist love.'

When she asks him to lay out the practice of his free love, he is unable. She asks him who else he is seeing, if he is seeing anyone she knows, anyone she loves. 'I don't want to be standing in a roomful of people who know something I don't. Please don't make a fool of me,' she says. 'I am what you are. I am open. I just want to know how to act. Is there anything you need to tell me?'

He shakes his head, 'No.'

November

What is this here in this Petri dish picture? We are in white lab coats, in the bodies of white men with large seeing-eye glasses with thin, wiry frames. We look at a recent image of a nearby galaxy caught in the swallowed flash of our earthling technologies. There, we read it away from ourselves. No more do the galaxies go through the belly (his fire) but through the brain.

'There's something lacking in the base. The ideological foundation is weak, there's an epistemic clarity missing. Your praxis has no ontological density,' Goitsi says, again reflecting, this time on the ethics of decolonial praxis in the classroom. 'There is a violence happening here that you are not willing to acknowledge,' to a fictional teacher existing in real time. 'I am a validating factor for your research. My experiential knowing, which you so question with well-meaning suspicion, lets these people know that you know what you are talking about – presented here, the Subject! The guinea pig spinning new ideological theorems from the site of the struggle itself – me! The worker bee buzzing away silently at capitalism's epistemic mind farm.'

I don't disagree. My feet are warm and clammy on the red brick. My back touches the glass pane of the door behind me. It is cool and shocking. 'There is no purpose.' I'm remembering this out loud for Goitsi's sake, this morning's clanging conversation having gotten in between the places where the bones test their density. 'There is no ethical judge who floats above us and gifts us the wrath of our fruitless human labour to be good. No, there is no divine punisher. But the point –'

'Yes, the point!' Goitsi ties a neat package to a period. 'The point is not that there is someone giving brownie points for goodness and coals in the Christmas sack for the wicked. The point is to still choose to be ethical!'

'Ethical both for self and simultaneously for community. The point is to choose to be good. And not this selective goodness that these niggahs outchea finna be calling street practice. Not this violent, hard shell of a thing. Choose to be good in your politics, in your collisions with the people in the places of struggle, in your practice of intimacy. There in the politics between the struggle to the intimacy, I will map out on your body the disappearing trails of starlight rushing through time, a path to being more human. I would be free with you. Open and wrathful. Crying and fighting. Radically soft. The practice of your (man)hood is counter-liberation.'

What are the ethics of a decolonial, pedagogical praxis where the world is the classroom? Where the knowledge is mined on the weighted words slipping off pillows when you refuse to kiss me goodnight and I tell you that is violent. When I have laid out to you the many worlds that fell through the pinhole of this string's theory and found me, a child there, tangled in mess, trying to separate the rope, the chain, the whip, the weight. Radical softness!

I find this phrase with you. Me, an anxious swell of nausea like black time oozing out through my pores, unmaking my insanity here to lay the math of my liberation with the delicate balancing of quantum equations. Here, to be myself in the pink of inside flesh that slits, spills and bleeds blackly to me. Here, radical and soft.

'I am trying to be free here, homie. In case you misunderstood. Thought here's a pretty fuck-thing to play with, meanwhile what are the ethics of your free love?'

October

It is late in October. Her housemate tells her that her lover has been dating their mutual friend who is white and middle class for over a year now. She is floored. She comes back home one night and sitting across from each other at their dining room table listening to jazz and rolling tobacco to smoke, her housemate tells her how she has figured it out.

'You both kept having this similar experience of this man who, quite frankly, seems like a narcissist. You'd tell me things and there'd be too much overlap – how he treats you, how closed he always is, his politics. So eventually, I asked her where her boyfriend works and then I knew. I'm telling you first because you seem to be in this polyamorous thing with him. They've been dating since before October last year and he uses race against her in a similar way to how he uses class against you.' She pauses and looks at her with meaning. 'There is no version of this where she doesn't find out.'

She will confront him, ask him for the truth and he will say to her, 'I have this . . . thing . . . fear . . . *Ja*, fear of doing further damage. Like FOMO but Fear of Doing Further Damage.'

This next part doesn't happen like this, but this is how she writes it.

'You accept that you have damaged me and left me.'

He cannot look at her.

'Please say it.' Her voice is coarse gravel.

'I have damaged you and left you.'

There is a deliberate and visible smashing and everything falls apart. *Kubi*. (It is wrecked.)

Epilogue: November

We are behind a glass window inside a Petri dish, like a film being played. The image again of an amorphous cosmos, still to our gaze. We watch the slow happening of things. We watch the stars' dust breathe its first breath as we laugh out loud together, Goitsi and I. We laugh at the things we have left behind in other men's beds, scattering like the apparatus of some failed experiment. Purposeless, there is no one watching but us. All we have is our compassion, our tendency towards goodness, and always our unconscious struggle towards the creation of this new human. We lock the cool of the shaded house behind us. And tumble forward, again, into the moment, into the dusk, into the collective unconscious.

~

Qondiswa James is a black, queer femme from rural Transkei in the Eastern Cape of South Africa. She is a theatre-maker, performance artist, film and theatre performer, writer and activist. Follow her on Instagram: @blqgrl.radikl.

Getting to Know Each Other

Dr Mary Hames

Letter writing has become a thing of the past. Social media with its immediate gratification has, in some ways, taken romance out of dating. However, in this situation, two people exchange emails and a narrative of possibilities and trepidation unfolds. The distance between them makes the conversation meander between doubt, lust and love, while erotic fantasy slips in between the getting-to-know-you moments. It creates such a different kind of anticipation, connection and passion.

13 February

Dearest Letitia,

What an experience the past two nights have been. Not in my wildest imagination could I conjure the way this would turn out. You have welcomed me into your life, your body, in every imaginable way. You are really a remarkable woman. I would never have dreamed how sexy, audacious, funny, hot and ... wet you could be. You smelled terrific and tasted delicious. I look forward to fun with you, to discover things, to play, shop for 'toys' and experiment!

This is just the beginning.

Love,

Miriam

16 February

Dearest Letitia,

It is almost two in the morning. I woke up and it is hard for me to get back to sleep. You have invaded my dreams again. I woke up with a strong need to talk to you, to reassure you that it is okay with me that you have those feelings. I can imagine that there is a mixture of emotions, expectations and, of course, trepidation. I too am filled with a kind of wonder about recent developments. I want to shout to the world that there is someone new in my life – and then I realise that I must walk with caution, I must walk softly and proceed slowly. I am surprised at my own intensity when I am thinking of you, but I am also scared to think way ahead. I really do not want to scare you and push you away. I love women. I honour and respect them. I would gladly step aside if you are not ready for a relationship.

Love,

Miriam

*

Dearest Letitia,

Must say I enjoy switching on the computer and seeing your name on the screen. It is so exciting getting to know you while you are on the other side of the world. I love the benefits of technology.

I do like celebrating women's achievements, but sometimes I think the honeymoon is becoming too extended. Maybe it's my age (oh yeah, at times I can be very ageist) and a combination of life experiences. My best friends are children and the aged. From

189

the first I'm taught how to live and love unconditionally, and from the latter I'm taught how to deal with life and let go. The last lesson can be extremely difficult but things have a way to fade with time and one tends to remember only the good and can laugh about the bad. I also believe that everyone that you meet has something to teach you and all the experiences you live through have the same goal. Did it make me a better person? I do not know, but when I look at my friendships – some longer than 30 years – then I say well done, you've chosen the best.

Maybe this sharing with you over the next couple of weeks will bring me to new insights. I hope you will start to trust me enough to also share about you and your thoughts, your ideals, your feelings. It is a strange thing – this getting to know each other. The breathlessness of anticipation, the wariness of: am I sharing too much too soon? The what if? Do I really want to? And so on.

I meant it when I said I would really like to know you better. You hold a certain kind of fascination for me. You're very interesting and strangely stubborn. So please keep on writing to me. It keeps me sane in my own mad world.

Take good care of yourself. Love yourself and think of me.

Love,

Miriam

*

22 February

Hi Miriam,

I really enjoyed your last email and also printed it. I have to admit it reminded me of Bessie Head's letters – shifts and turns and sudden highs of intimacy. About what you say, I really agree with you, but mainly theoretically because I still find it so hard to let go of silly stuff, even when I know it hurts me, and to really, really relax and have fun, though when I do, I really like it and wonder why I don't do it more often and more readily. I think you let things go easily from what I've seen, and wondered why you once (quite a while ago) said you are scared of looking within, when it seems you so very often do but aren't fazed.

I think I'm learning more now how to live in the moment but still need to 'train' myself away from old habits. I'm impatient and self-absorbed and my thoughts are always all over the place – in the future (or past) – so I forget to enjoy what's now. Which is why I really value yoga and am fascinated by eastern philosophy – it trains me away from my bad habits and makes me realise how much there is to gain from slowing down and relaxing. Now that I've started 'waxing lyrical', I'm tempted to go on and on. (Hope you are not already looking at the length of this email with dismay – oh my God, look what she's written, now I need to reply and I really have to? I'm very paranoid and self-conscious.) To get back to waxing lyrical though, it may be the distance and writing thing. Anyway, the other thing is also what you said, about being anxious about what to say / when to say / how far / how much.

Let me stop here. I took your advice last night.

Love love love,

Letitia

*

26 February

Hello Letitia,

I wish you would have continued 'waxing lyrical'. For the first time, I felt that you were opening up about yourself. I saw a glimpse of the inner you, it is tantalising, very provocative, teasing . . .

You told me that you'd purchased a pair of purple jeans. What shade of purple are the jeans? Does the colour have a specific meaning for you? I love the colour purple and every time I notice it somewhere – a flower, the bougainvillea, a speck in the veld, a wall, a dress, just about anything – I embrace it. The warmth, the meaning, the potential it holds. This afternoon I attended my Women and Spirituality class. It is fun. I enjoy it. I do think it is time to get back to school full time for at least a year. I am tired of educating myself and need some interaction with others. Ideas must be shared to be worthwhile.

Do you really think I let go of things easily? No, honey, it usually takes a long time of anxiety, of thinking all kinds of weird thoughts, such as what have I done wrong, why does it always happen to me, do I love too much, did I become too dependent? And all that jazz. It does become easier with time. Each time it is different. This time the pain was shorter because I had a feeling it was over long ago and it would have been stupid of me to cling on to something I had no control over.

So, talking about being paranoid, that is me. I just camouflage it well. You can write me a book, hundreds of pages. Must talk to me, share with me. Let me know you on a different level. (One fantasy of mine is that you are reading me your favourite poetry.

Will it remain a fantasy?) I sometimes wish I had the gift to let the words flow and weave into memorable poetry/songs/stories. I want to tell the world how I feel, but usually every thought ends up dead in my head and never ends up on paper. I live in my head most of the time. I can be lost and lonely in a crowd. I dissect and analyse inside of me and that is why I am sometimes scared to look too hard within.

Take care, dress warm, look after that cold.

Love,

Miriam

*

26 February

Dearest Miriam,

Strange week with lots of running around and not much done. Funny how wonderful 'home' is when you're away from it. You mentioned spirituality classes before, and I'd love to know what you do. My spiritual thing is only vaguely Buddhist since I don't do much reading/practice in relation to this. Want to follow up more. I do think you camouflage well, but I also see that you live in your head a bit (a lot), though thought this was with more detachment than you said. But you're contradictory – I have a sense of you being really 'wild' (have heard much about your 'wild parties') and yet also shy. Reclusive and even introverted (confirmed by some things said but really my observation). Think I am this too. I do like opening up with you though and thought I had started to do so before the last email (don't just mean sex). I'd love to sing to you really – not only recite poetry – I know what

I'd sing too. I also live in my head quite weirdly sometimes and when I get out, realise the world's NOT AT ALL what I was thinking – usually much easier, far less fraught than I was imagining. I looove purple, for reasons you give too. But these days I am veering towards deep red and mustardy-yellow. This email is a bit unsatisfactory. Would like to phone and think I will but would be nice to do on the spur of the moment (if that's okay with you). Will take a chance.

Thinking of you.

A lot.

Love love love,

Letitia

*

5 March

My dearest Letitia,

A sigh of relief. I like writing you. I'm constantly composing letters in my head and have long conversations with you. This is amazing because a few weeks ago I thought that I may never be able to like/love somebody. I was so sure that my relationship in the recent past would last forever. Alas some things became unbridgeable. We found it even too difficult to speak about the divides. This is enough for now.

When you first crossed my path, I saw it as a challenge and to my great surprise I felt something stir deep inside of me. It was as if something started to slowly peel away. I became wary and scared. The first thought was that you wanted to experiment, that you wanted to feel what it was like to be with a woman. I, the adventurer, thought nothing of taking the plunge, but in the aftermath I realised that I may be capable of hurting you deeply. That is why I was so concerned about keeping you away from the rumours, the 'crowd'. I very seldom socialise in those circles. I keep my own and follow my own drum beat. I'm really a very private person, sometimes to my own detriment.

I want to write you a thousand times a day. I want to share with you what I read. I want to know what you like, the food, the movies, the kind of friends/people, the books you read, the poems, the kind of holidays you would like to go on. About my-self . . . mmmm let me see . . . I'm an eclectic reader from silly sex books to anything that I want to know about from politics to re-ligion. Sometimes I think that life is too short for me to be able to read them all.

Sleep well lover.

All my love,

Miriam

*

Hi Miriam,

This is a quickie. Want to talk. Why are you being so alarmist? Why do you think you could hurt me??? Why do you think I could hurt you??? I am glad you are not part of the 'dyke commu-nity'. Let's talk on Sunday. I am not just curious, want to under-stand why you are so worried, concerned at the same time as pleased and happy.

Much love,

Letitia

6 March

Dearest Letitia,

Sometimes the tongue is mightier than the pen. So, let's talk on Sunday. Looking forward and counting the time. If I sounded like the goddess of doom, I apologise. Just so paranoid sometimes and I really have moved from my original perceptions – in fact quite a distance. Please be patient with me. Told you I'm a mess. All my love (mean it!)

Miriam

*

6 March

Hi Miriam,

I want to find a word for you that really conveys how I feel – have experimented but none work so far, so for me there's an incredible pleasure in your name. Wonder if you'll get this before we talk . . . Having quite a good weekend but popped in to see if you'd written. Just want to say for now, have been thinking nothing but positive things re: you. Really. No anxiety, fear in relation to you and others. So, I'm self-centred and not really hearing when you raise these. You make me feel happy (more than that, blissful), energised, content and safe and optimistic – all at once. And when I think of you, whatever else I'm thinking/ doing is transformed somehow, and I want to smile. Or move around like a joyful child, or just lie down and feel amazing waves of feeling. One fantasy (mentioned before) keeps popping up – dancing with you to Buena Vista Social Club – don't know why

I'm obsessed with this. Anyway, so though you have told me some things about yourself and others (and this is the kind of pain I really have never experienced), I don't fully understand. But I so want you to feel like I do. Talk soon – if you get this before we talk, that is.

Love love love.

Letitia

*

10 March

Dearest Letitia,

I enjoyed the unexpected call. While I was otherwise occupied, I thought of you but was too scared to let you know. Afraid that I would push you away by making any concrete suggestions. Now I can at least visualise doing things with you. And yes, I'll go to X with you. This is a promise unless you get pissed off with me. I'll email the organiser tomorrow.

But back to us? I think you are a witch and you've waved your magic wand over me. I keep thinking of you and no matter what kind of shitty day I had, the thought of you dispels all kinds of nonsense. I just want to bask in the dreams about you. When I saw a photo of you today, my heart missed a beat. I feel so much tenderness when I think of you. I want to caress you, hold you. I look forward to not having to come home or rush off to work after I've been with you. I will schedule a day's leave when you get back.

Your name is like honey on my tongue. I want to repeat it over and over. I want to roll my tongue all over your back. I want to cover your body with mine. I want to leave the light on when we make love. I want you to tell me stories in the aftermath and then hold you while you sleep.

You have become my deepest desire.

Love

As always,

Miriam

*

10 March

Dear dear Miriam,

How to use words to convey the way I feel? Don't know. Wish I could touch you, whisper in your ear, stroke your legs, kiss your breasts, play with your hair, listen to your laugh, feel your chest vibrating when you say 'mmmmmmm', wake up and see you there, watch you do little things you don't know I see but really treasure – like standing at the kitchen counter gently smiling, waiting for the kettle to boil to make tea. Small moments – wonderful moments. Don't think you know what these mean to me. You MUST know I more than 'like you a lot' – don't know this feeling but am finding it wonderful. I wish I could show you in ways that feel better – looking, smiling, touching, playing, doing small things ... But agree there is something about this distance allowing us to communicate in different ways, that we're weirdly having an opportunity to grow towards each other. One thing I always mean to ask, do you ever think about the stones???? Really don't know why I collected those stones and brought them back at the time – strange impulse I definitely didn't think about then. And the fact that I didn't, for example, while packing in the hotel, simply dump them. Strange thing . . .

How weird your recollection of the evening you brought me home . . . Didn't know what was on your mind at all. Just thought you were keen to get home . . . Truly. I am not being coy. Thought again you were laughing at me somehow because I was trying to find out if you were free the next Saturday and you were looking for something and I had to ask a second time and you said in a way I thought was indulgently impatient that yes, you would come. Felt foolish.

Really needed to talk to you last night and soooo glad I got through. By the way, shall I phone again on Sunday evening or another time?

Take care,

Letitia

*

11 March

Dearest Letitia

Honey,

I just shared with someone the other day that the ancestors must have spoken to you and sent you to bring me those stones. I kept the bigger one for myself as a constant reminder of the gift you brought. If we believe in deeper meanings of life then that could be true. You were the unexpected gift . . . And you're a very special gift to me.

The more I know about you the more the feelings of contentment. (I fear that I've got a constant musky smell because my panty gets wet every time I think of you). You're always on my mind and many times I'm not aware of my surroundings. I think of you coming back ... When you asked me to go with you to the conference ... I realised that it is only happening in October and I had the feeling that you're asking me for some kind of future commitment. You were hesitant though ... Saying that even as a friend I can tag along. I do plan to go ... Though not 'only as a friend' ... As a 'lover' perhaps and, to be more specific, 'your loved one'? Not only to be with you but also to share space with all the writers who are displayed on my bookshelves.

Imagine Maya Angelou, Hurston, Walker and others. It would be an amazing experience and you should keep me from gushing. I intend to buy books, books, books ....

I am falling deeply in love with you as a person. There is something in you that is unpretentious, sexy, warm, bubbly, caring ... All the things you hide behind a cool exterior. For me it is such a pleasure to peel the layers and every time discover something new. You are leaving me breathless ...

You talk about the little things you've noticed, so have I. Your head on my shoulder, sitting on my lap, taking my hand and placing it between your legs. How I loved to kiss you there. The look in your eyes when you're spent ... The smile on your face. The last night/morning you really kissed me when I had to leave. I so much wanted to stay and would have but I had that stupid workshop the next day.

I could go on and on. I think you've said what I wanted to hear in your email, and I am prepared to take the quantum leap.

Keep well, my love.

As always,

Miriam

11 March

Miriam Miriam Miriam,

What can I call you? I want to find a name so I'm testing in my head different ones, but for now to enjoy 'Miriam'. Different things to say today ... But really wanted to call all evening and somehow felt you would, though didn't expect it to be so late. It was a wonderful surprise. I'm glad you told me about your experience. By now you must know how I feel. I want you to know it's beyond words. I love you. Everything about you. And you really don't know, I think, how much of this has to do with images/impressions you don't know I see – things you don't really know or see about yourself. Maybe your incredible gentleness and warmth, your incredible shyness, your sense of bemusement and confusion when something is going on around you and you're really taking it in and wanting to comment and sometimes start but not following it through, things about you that make me almost see you as a little girl. You are not confrontational or aggressive at all. I think I am more so than you. Your sense of humour, your incredible laugh, which makes me think of who you are sexually, emotionally and intellectually (if that makes sense) all at once. I loooove your breasts, your hands, your calves, the soft mound between your legs, the shape and feel of your buttocks, your smile and the murmuring sounds you make, make me want to swooooon (not only nineteenth century ladies do this). Your hands, your picking lavender and ever-so-carefully tying it into bunches for me. The way you tidy up all the time, not frantically like most people do, but as though you need to take care of everything you touch. A memory of you – kneeling over me, reaching up to push back your hair with your head thrown back and your beautiful breasts above my face. Wanted to touch and kiss them so much but was so scaaared, didn't know what to touch or how, so stuck, as you no doubt noticed, to one thing – not very adventurously too! Thought you would find me clumsy and gauche. Don't care now if you do. Want to enjoy your body anyway.

Love love love,

Letitia

*

17 March

Hi Miriam,

For me it was absolutely essential that we talked last night and, as I said, I really wanted to BE WITH YOU. Wanted to hear your laugh right next to me, wanted to see your smile, look sort of at me but also beyond, wanted to feel your body vibrating when you say 'mmmmmmm'. Wanted to hold your hand, play with your hair and kiss your neck, your breasts, wanted to hug you really tightly and feel we had endless evenings together to do desultory things on the spur of the moment.

Something that we must also talk about is the 'power stuff'.

BUT ... all that definitely NOT foremost in my mind. Am happy, ecstatic, over the moon to feel the way I feel about you, I am over the moon you feel the way you feel for me, I am over the moon to think we will see each other again soon. Fantasise endlessly about what we'll do and making a trip to hot springs almost immediately after I get back.

Know that you will force me to laugh at silly things about myself, for one, and help me not to be complacent but also encourage me when I need it – all that at a very practical level. But other immeasurable things to do with how one somehow expands, throbs, swells when one loves a person, that is quite impossible for me to define.

Will probably be travelling when you read this ... Of course, I will try to email you. Of course. Because I want to. Otherwise, will call you on Wednesday or Thursday – will keep trying until I find you, so please do not 'synchronise your times'.

Love you lots and lots and lots,

Letitia

*

27 March

Hi Letitia

Your email today ... So ambiguous – especially the part where you shared that you have flirted with B ... Be assured that is natural, it feels good – the more mature side of me said it is okay. Then there is the other side of me – not jealous – but discomfort. This is my truth. It is good that you have shared this with me. I also flirt a lot – it does not necessarily mean that I want to pursue somebody, but it makes me feel alive, wanted and human.

Hey, I am still waiting on your call. Please call tonight. I would love to hear your voice.

Love,

Miriam

*

29 March

Dearest Miriam,

I found our talk yesterday quite difficult, and know I did not (and often do not) give satisfactory responses, explanations etc. Difficult but important for me to think where we are going. I hope you feel as safe about exploring, getting to know me as I do in relation to you.

Talking on the phone is also a bit disappointing in terms of my communicating to you how I feel, what I want, what I like – in all ways. With normal conversations, we could talk for hours, and there'd be breaks, and time to get back to something, and follow up the very next day with more long talks, or phone on impulse, and so on, but one- to two-hour phone calls per week is frustrating. Still, I don't want to stop the calls of course. I would like so much to tell you exactly, in precise detail, how I feel when I think about you, how I feel swollen, charged, soft, restful all at the same time, about my fantasies about you, not simply that 'I want you on/behind my back', but exactly what – coming into a room and undressing you slowly without you seeing me before and then not looking at me during (so I could watch and enjoy the way you register how you feel), dancing with you to Buena Vista Social Club music (here comes my old fantasy again – and feeling I am leading you and am totally absorbed by my movement together with you), kneeling between your legs and slowly spreading your thighs, kissing your inner thighs, then holding you and moving you up and down first gently and slowly and then faster ... sucking and licking your fingers and stroking them wet over my breasts, kissing and sucking your breasts and feeling your wetness all over my legs, my back, my face . . . Pulling myself up onto your lap, feeling you licking and sucking my breasts . . .

I hope that you will allow me to get to know you better and trust that I want more than virtual interaction, titillating oral sex and abstract fantasy . . .

All my love,

Letitia

*

31 March

Dear Letitia,

I wish I could consult a looking glass. I wish I could see what the future holds. Am I the one who fears commitment? Deep down inside of me I am still shocked, painfully hurt, afraid to love so deeply and completely so soon after my previous relationship. I was devastated after the last breakup. I so believed that my love for her would be able to transcend everything, and then she threw me a curve ball. Tonight, I feel it. I have got this incredible pressure on my chest. I can't breathe properly – I've got to let it go. I also feel the pressure from you. I read your mail and feel the hidden messages. I feel your need to love, to depend, to rely on, and I am shit scared. Would I be able to live up to your expectations? Did I push too far too soon?

Miriam

~

Dr Mary Hames is the director of the University of the Western Cape's Gender Equity Unit.

Dangerous Deities

Wanelisa Xaba

'I never knew God until the night I had a Black woman's face between my thighs, to be honest,' she says as her lips create an O around the neck of her Black Label. I want to tell her many things. I want to tell her she is a flip-flopper. Just last week she told me she doesn't believe in God. I want to scream at her. Can she not see that women who drink Black Label, wear black lipstick, smoke Stuyvesant Red and find deities between other Black girls' thighs don't live to see 30 in South Africa?

'But I don't know man . . . ' she continues before I get a chance to say anything back. 'With men it was easier. If men rejected me, I knew how to brick myself into a solid wall. Yes, I'd come out of it harder. But I'd come out of it, you know?! With women, I just can't . . . ' Her black lips create a black O around the Black Label again. Her throat moves up and down like an empty elevator. She places the Black Label near her heart.

'I just can't handle the rejection. How do you live when God has rejected you? The God who is oso your image? I guess it is part of "adulting", neh? To live with disappointment. To smile and reply, "I'm good, thanks," when the pit of your stomach is a liquid furnace. To stand in front of big crowds and tell them life is worth living, then go home and masturbate until you cry. Because you only want the God and your hands have become refugees to your skin. You want the God. You want the Black woman. Yet her heart is elusive like the dreams you have half-asleep and half-awake on a chair on a Sunday afternoon. The God. It is not that she is not built for love, she is just lost. You cannot worship inside a temple with no foundation. But fuck it, I have never wanted to build a home in the middle of a sea storm so badly. I want to place a prayer mat in the middle of a volcano eruption and pray to her.'

'Now that is your issue,' I tell her. 'Black women are not Gods. They are very close though. They can only be Gods if our notions of Godliness is stretched to accommodate brokenness. But we don't find beauty in brokenness, do we? Which is strange because we are so good at breaking each other. So give that Black woman who broke you her humanity. Allow Black women their humanity. There is nothing noble about being a God in an anti-God society.'

～

Wanelisa Xaba is a PhD student and Black feminist writer. She holds a Bachelor of Social Sciences degree and an Honours degree in African Studies. She pursued a master's by research at the University of Cape Town. She has also documented LGBTQI hate crimes in South Africa with Iranti-org. In 2017, she was named as one of the *Mail and Guardian*'s 200 influential young South Africans.

Stigma, Shame and Sex Work

Noluvuyo Zaza

Trigger warning: rape

I was 23 when I arrived in Cape Town; I had travelled from my hometown, King William's Town in the Eastern Cape, for a new life in the Mother City. I wanted to be closer to jobs, I wanted to be closer to opportunities, and I wanted to be closer to everything that I did not have access to back home. I'd left home because I could not stand the stigma of being HIV positive anymore. I was diagnosed with HIV when I was eighteen years old. A year before, I had fallen in love with a man and I carried his child and gave birth to a healthy baby girl. She is twelve years old now. When I found out that I was HIV positive, I was shocked. I did not expect it at all and because I knew that stigma and negative attitudes would follow me wherever I went, I made the decision to keep it to myself. However, in 2013, my boyfriend and the father of my child passed away. I became fearful again; I thought I was also going to die. Everyone in the village knew that the cause of his death was because he was also HIV positive. I knew that if I were to stay in my community I would have to face everyone again – their questions and their curiosity. I had to say goodbye to friends who did not want anything to do with me anymore. I had to let go of people who I thought were dear to me. Many of them stopped wanting me around all because of my positive status so I packed my belongings for a life in Cape Town.

Things in Cape Town were not what I expected. I thought everything was supposed to be easier in the big cities, but life was difficult. Where were the jobs? Where was the money? Where were the opportunities? I struggled to find a job in the first couple of months; it was tough. I had *no* money coming in and this affected me greatly. After a couple of months, I was hopeless. During this time, I made new friends and we would go out together and drink and dance to have a good time. Sometimes we would have sex with different people and sometimes we would have sex with them for beers. I had been doing sex work before I called myself a sex worker without even knowing it. Then one day, I met someone who became my girlfriend and introduced me to the sex-work industry. Since then, I have been a sex worker and I like my job; it gives me freedom. Since becoming a sex worker, things finally started to become better as I could take care of myself.

In the last couple of years, I have realised a lot of things. Firstly, I am a lesbian – I love women. This was a big challenge for me to accept. I didn't know what was happening to me. I didn't know who to speak to about my sexuality. Secondly, I have realised that women's clothing was not something I enjoyed dressing myself in. People in my community would call me names. They would call me *nkonkoni* (lesbian) and I have been raped and robbed multiple times because of my sexuality and the work that I do. I have endured violence and shame. I have lost family and friends because of my sexuality. At times, even my clients are judgmental. They will say things like, 'But you are a man, I don't want a man.' Then they will go find someone else to provide the service. This doesn't bother me that much as clients like different things on different nights. Some nights they want me, some nights they want someone different.

A year ago, I was raped and the Sex Workers Education & Advocacy Taskforce (SWEAT), the organisation I am a part of, placed me in contact with Mothers for the Future – a group of mothers who are sex workers who provide training, responsible parenting classes, speakers, resources like nappies, and everything we need to live a supported life. They sent me home to take time to heal. SWEAT has provided me with so much support over the years.

People in our communities do not understand us and they use our identities as a reason to hurt us. People in our communities do not think lesbians are 'women enough' and think that being lesbian means you want to label yourself as a man. This means that there is a gap in the understanding of our community in the areas where we live. The South African government should dispense more information to communities about being a part of the Lesbian, Gay, Bisexual, Transgender, Intersex, being Queer and here, and plus community so that we can remove the stigma and the brutal violence that still follows us around wherever we go. The South African government should decriminalise sex work so that we, as sex workers, can have access to healthcare, so that the police will listen to us when we say we have faced violence at the hands of the community and clients, so that our children can be raised with an emotionally pain-free experience of life, so that we can make money, rent our own apartments to provide our services in spaces that are safer for us as sex workers, and raise our children in an environment where we do not constantly face the fear of being arrested for providing a service just like all other working parents and people strive to do.

~

Noluvuyo Zaza is a proud lesbian and sex worker.

I Now Breathe

Khanya Kemami

From a young age, I was constantly told to be myself and that I'm allowed to live freely and to breathe deeply. I always felt I knew what that meant: I am allowed to be as lesbian and as masculine as I'd like.

Throughout my life, I was considered the confident one, the one who knew themselves better than anyone could – I was *self-aware Khanya*. Teenage me always knew their sexuality and had been vividly, rather aggressively, masculine-appearing and vocal about their attraction to women and Queer men. I was always wearing my Queerness first. I was also the only (loudly) openly Queer kid in high school, never felt intimidated by it or ever felt it was up for discussion with my peers. The brave, intimidating, self-confident and aggressive Queer kid was my entire aesthetic and my reputation, although another part of me never felt it wholeheartedly.

I'd always felt 'half' myself. I hesitated before being assertive and my chest tightened when I had to speak about myself. I was shaky in my description and unsure about my delivery, my appearance, my voice, the way I stood, the tone of my voice – just unsure of 'me'. I avoided and avoided and avoided thinking about it.

Thinking about it became easier to avoid when I turned seventeen. I got really good at drowning my thoughts by drinking cheap liquor and getting into fights at bars we weren't allowed to be in. Nothing felt like it would change, so thinking more about myself took a back seat.

Then nineteen hit and one of my very good friends, we'll call them Kitten, said to me, 'If I ever transitioned, would you hate me?' *Transition?* That was the very first time I'd ever heard of the term 'transitioning', and I will admit I didn't fully understand what he meant but I knew I wouldn't hate him for taking control of his body and carrying on in life as he chose to. As time progressed, I came to learn that he was 'transgender' and the process of 'transitioning' was him basically masculinising his appearance to achieve a more male appearance. This was when I developed an envy towards him but why, I thought? I wasn't sure at the time, but hell, I was so envious. For years I felt this whilst he transitioned and never questioned it any further.

I regret never questioning it further.

A few years later at 22, or what I call 'my breaking age', was when the thoughts I'd been trying so long to avoid became incredibly unavoidable. I lost my ability to breathe, to love myself or even see myself as an adult. I was me and my body was a separate entity I dragged along, never feeling emotion from the touch of others. Whether it be a hug from my parents or the romantic embrace of my partner, I felt nothing. I was in a constant state of numbness and the worse part was that I had finally let myself think about it all and came to terms with the reason I felt this way. Now the issue was that I didn't feel brave enough to say it out loud. I felt like I had no right to be myself after denying myself for so long. I had wasted my chance. It was over. I thought: *Khanya, you can never ever tell them. It's too late. They won't love you, you'll fuck everything up. You've made your bed, so lie in it.*

22 October 2018 is the day I wanted to die. It's all I wanted, felt and thought about. I premeditated and planned my departure and I was not going to leave a note. I was going to do it in my room while everyone slept so when they woke up it'd be like I'd died in my sleep. I thought it'd be better. Ultimately, I would have rather taken my own life than confront the truth – purely because I was afraid of being disowned or being unloved. I had avoided the truth for so long, so so long, I started believing I was content in being and dying as a woman, when in reality I was draining the life out of myself, stunting my growth and affecting my breathing. Little did I know my avoidance was a ticking time bomb waiting to detonate. It became too much, my decision was made, I wouldn't make it to 23.

On 4 November 2018, I'd been crying for two days and hadn't eaten for the past three. I was aching but I could finally feel my body for once. It felt awful but I didn't care to change it. I felt helpless, weak and didn't see value in any of this.

My mother knocked on my bedroom door and peeked her head in, 'Nana, you'll be okay, okay?' She said, 'I love you, we all love you, okay?'

I didn't know if she knew, maybe some kind of mother's intuition but those words she said were the reason I got up that night, walked to her room, tears cascading down my face, and came out to her and my father. Telling them I am a transgender man, I am not a woman and have never felt like one, I'm a man and would like to start hormone therapy. Thanks to her, for the second time, I took my first breath and started living. Thanks to her I found out I really am loved unconditionally and saw the extent of the love my African parents have for me.

It's 2019, I'm turning 23 in two months and am celebrating my third month on testosterone in a week's time. Now I breathe deeply and without shame, I feel and love my body and, most importantly, I fear dying. I don't avoid thinking about myself, if anything, I think a lot more about myself.

Living the life of a transgender child who lacked the language to express themselves was an extremely dark period. Although I had the unconditional love, never having the words can make being yourself and asserting it seem unattainable. I'm grateful for how everything has turned out for me but now I see the importance of accessible LGBTQIA+ information, the importance to speak freely about it, the importance of positive representation within the community and the importance of self-love in Queer children of colour. We should all be allowed to live freely, love deeply and breathe even deeper.

At the age of 22, I have finally started living and I never want to give it up.

∽

Khanya Kemami is a Queer South African illustrator and graphic artist based in Johannesburg. Follow them on Instagram: @the.peng.qing

Stripped

Kelly Smith

The first time I took off my clothes on stage, it wasn't to read out loud from a book. Neither were the second or third times. But after two years of stripping out of burlesque costumes, I started stripping to tell stories.

My foray into burlesque began innocently enough – someone I hardly knew had a discount voucher for burlesque classes up for grabs. When I looked at the details, I discovered the classes were happening in my block, which was an old factory building converted mostly into apartments and also, apparently, a dance studio that I didn't even know existed. I went having zero idea that burlesque is a subculture that is the domain of dance performance artists with phenomenal costuming skills, gender-bending tendencies, and incurable addictions to glitter. I got sucked in instantly. But after years of taming my stage fright, memorising group choreography, mastering quick-changes backstage into different coloured garters and fishnet stockings, making my own nipple tassels, styling my thick curls into victory rolls and painting my face with vampish, red lips and perfectly-lined cat eyes, I bowed out. I decided it just wasn't for me while simultaneously being flabbergasted that I wasn't deriving pleasure from dancing, an activity I'd actively sought out for pleasure for as long as I could remember.

I've always loved dancing but my early years of dancing weren't spent warming up at the beam or learning choreography from a tattooed taskmaster for slick, professional theatre productions. They were spent sweaty and happy in crop tops and platform shoes on nightclub dance floors, in a bikini top and shorts at outdoor festivals, or just in jeans and Converse at house parties and dives.

Queer nightclubs were actually my first contact with Cape Town's queer community when I was in my teens, but oddly, it was straight friends who took me there – friends who knew someone who had a car or had a car themselves, which was very valuable friendship currency in the pre-Uber days unless you'd prefer to take the first Metrorail train or minibus taxi home at 6 am in your party outfit. The heyday of queer clubs and bars like Angels and Bronx are long gone but I vividly remember the feeling of belonging I felt in those queer spaces. Where you came from didn't matter. It was where us misfits got to play after our waitressing shifts ended, where tried and trusted dealers and drag queens were always in arm's reach, where the barmen were always topless, music was playing seven days a week, and the toilets smelled like Jeyes Fluid and blow jobs. It may not sound glamorous but these spaces were packed to the rafters until sunrise on weekends and weekdays alike – a refuge for the restless, the misunderstood and the horny.

Burlesque was, it turned out, my stepping stone to producing a performance art event called Naked Girls Reading. It was also a boot camp for getting my boobs out, a training ground for my temerity, and fortification for all of my female anatomy to become accustomed to being scrutinised by an audience. Basically, it was the baptism of fire I needed to even contemplate getting involved in something where it was a prerequisite to not have a stitch of clothing on in front of a roomful of strangers. In retrospect, maybe I never reached a full level of comfort on the burlesque stage because teasing using my body isn't actually my style. I've always teased with my words, my suggestions, my inappropriate jokes, my innuendoes that you belong in my bed and you should come and find out why. Sure, I'd be flattered to see your eyes on my hips while I danced in front of you but I'd be more satisfied with leaving you speechless with a flirtatious quip that gave you a peep into my dirty mind. And mine brimmed with ideas and stories I wanted to share that would pique interest in one way or another.

Just as writers can be consumed by jealousy reading a piece they wished they'd written themselves, when I stumbled across the concept of Naked Girls Reading, I wished I was the one who'd dreamed it up. So simple, yet so provocative: completely naked women reading literature aloud. I applied for the license to be the producer of the Cape Town chapter in 2014 and happily joined an international tribe – the event happens in 25 cities around the world.

Naked Girls Reading is a sexy book club, a living breathing nude painting and a sumptuously scandalous gathering all at once. But the mind fuck that no one ever sees coming is that the nudity turns out to be secondary to the readings. It is a constantly revolving wheel of forgetting and remembering that the women on stage are unclothed because the alchemy of the words is potent enough to make that enticing detail just slip away as quickly and as easily as we disrobe.

I use my book as my armour against any skittishness I may feel about being nude. Instead, I focus on the words on the page and harness their distracting power to transport roomfuls of people away into the theatre of the mind.

Disrobing together with the rest of the cast is my absolute favourite moment; the entire audience holding their breath as we give them permission to look at our naked bodies is palpable. It's both powerful and disarming, our nervousness sometimes apparent and surprisingly endearing. I think about how women do this at events across four continents and how I wish I could attend and read in them all – around the world in eighty disrobes, a dizzying feat of baring myself in different countries to have people listen to words, consider perspectives, and relate to original concepts they may not even know exist. But most of all, we do this to share tangles of letters that make people feel less alone. Not a pimping out of the body and mind, but rather language and the tales told used to soothe, placate, ignite, and touch another without lifting a finger to their skin.

I live for the surprise of the blatant eroticism being surpassed by ideas and imagination, and the unexpected truth that a story can have the power to draw their gaze away from our glorious nakedness blindsides the audience every time. There are probably scenarios that I am not privy to being weaved in audience members' minds that could both arouse and repulse me but that's not the point.

Out of all the stories I love to read, the queer ones are my favourite. The stories and articles and poems allow entry into my world, a world people may know nothing about but ultimately end up having their hearts open up to, like when the reading of *Queer Poetics: How to Make Love to a Trans Person* by Gabe Moses[28] made a straight woman stop me after the show to tell me that listening to it made her want to start kissing the stranger sitting next to her and how she imagined the whole room following suit, moved by the beautiful words:

> 'Realize that bodies are only a fraction of who we are
> They're just oddly-shaped vessels for hearts
> And honestly, they can barely contain us.'

Or the satisfaction I get from the ode to butch women and the desire conveyed in the physical descriptions taken from Tristan Taormino's *Of Butches, Kings and Masculinity*[29]:

> 'I love butch girls. Girls with slick, shiny, barbershop haircuts, trimmed so short your fingertips can barely grip it. Girls with shirts that button the other way. Girls that swagger ... Girls who get stared at in the ladies' room, girls who shop in the boys' department, girls who love every moment looking like they weren't supposed to. Girls with hands that touch me like they have been

28 *Wild Gender*. 7 May 2012. http://wildgender.com/queer-poetics-how-to-make-love-to-a-trans-person. Last accessed 26 May 2019.
29 Taormino, T. 5 October 1999. Of Butches, Kings, and Masculinity. *Village Voice*. http://www.villagevoice.com/1999-10-05/columns/of-butches-kings-and-masculinity/ Archived, no longer available.

exploring my body their entire lives ... It is the girls that get called sir every day who make me catch my breath, the girls with strong jaws who buckle my knees, the girls who are a different gender who make me want to lay down for them.'

I can feel my desire radiate out into the crowd and get absorbed when I read that excerpt. Its content is perfectly countered by the acknowledgement of the invisibility of the femme lesbian in Ivan E. Coyote's classic *Hats Off (to beautiful femmes)*[30] where this message never fails to hit home for women who think their sexuality goes unnoticed and unappreciated:

'I want to thank you for coming out of the closet. Again and again, over and over, for the rest of your life. At school, at work, at your kid's daycare, at your brother's wedding, at the doctor's office. Thank you for sideswiping their stereotypes. I never get the chance to come out of the closet, because my closet was always made of glass. But you do it for me. You fight homophobia in a way that I never could. Some of them think I am queer because I am undesirable. You prove to them that being queer is your desire.'

I revel in the discomfort of the audience, their slow revealing realisations and the ultimate empathy created by many of the readings. Especially Unoma Azuah's *The Choke of Grief*[31] – a

30 Coyote, I. 2011. *Persistence: All Ways Butch and Femme*. Arsenal Pulp Press: Vancouver.

31 Animashaun & Iradukunda & Kimutai & Muranda & Speaks. 2016. *Walking The Tightrope: Poetry and Prose by LGBTQ Writers from Africa*. Tincture / Lethe Press: New Jersey.

dedication to the victims and survivors of 'corrective rape', that ungodly crime where lesbians are raped in an attempt to 'rectify' their homosexuality but more often than not ends in our murder. It never fails to make those listening as well as those reading weep as the list of names goes on and on and seems never-ending because it is. The haunting words of non-queer listeners follow afterwards, quietly admitting, 'We just had no idea ... We didn't know it was that bad.'

If I have to use my naked body to make queerness or simply lifestyles, opinions and perceptions other than your own accessible, I'll do it a million times over. Some may call my nudity a gimmick but I call it a means-to-an-end, a method to the madness, and a stripper's reveal turned revelation, one that peels away prejudice and goes far beyond skin deep.

∼

Kelly Smith is a Capetonian jack-of-all-trades and master of fun – curator of the Cape Town chapter of international literary performance art event Naked Girls Reading and hostess of The Unofficial Pink Party, a celebration of the LGBTQI community.

Return to Sender

Zoey Black

For trans girls, wherever they may be.

Dear little Zo,

It's been over twenty years. I'm sorry it's taken so long to write you.

There have been days where I've wanted to tell you all the things and remake the world for you. There have been weeks where I've forgotten the flow of your long black curls and the shade of your sunshine yellow dress. And the years went by and you had to figure it out on your own – figure out all of this, all the things I never said . . . the things I should've told you.

I should've told you that it was going to be hard. That it was going to be the hardest thing you've ever had to do, that you've ever had to live through, and live with. That there will be days you'll be laughed at, whispered about, and teased and bullied. That at the end of those days, you'd cry yourself to sleep. That you won't want to get out of bed and face the pounding of fists that repeat from the day and weeks before. It's going to be hard.

I should've told you.

I should've told you that you'd feel like you don't belong. That you'd feel like an outsider because you were living outside yourself for so long. That you'd struggle to connect with others because you'd muted from connecting with who you are.

I should've told you that you don't need to be perfect in order to be loved. That you didn't need to perform or pretend or play a role to be accepted. That you didn't need to hide your short-comings or beat yourself up because you weren't enough. That you didn't need to silence your voice for the sake of someone else's.

I should've told you that you'd hit rock bottom. That you'd completely fall apart. That you'd shatter. That the pieces would never fit back together. That you would cut your fingers as you try to piece together the broken bits of yourself. That you will be changed. Forever. That you will experience violence. That your body will be targeted and policed. That you will be at the mercy of their words and their fists. That you will be pulled into dark corners, stripped bare and torn apart. That you will have to hide to be safe.

I should've told you it's not your fault. I should've told you that it gets better. That you will work harder than you ever have before to make it alright. That the work will be worth it. That you will remake yourself from the fire and the elements. That you will be a force of nature. That the world will look at you and be consumed with the power of your being. That you will inspire people. That your courage is real and acknowledged. That your bravery and honesty is a medicine. That you will go on to do great things, and that what you thought was impossible, is right at your fingertips.

I should've told you that you will find a family. That they will cook you the most delicious home-cooked dinners and buy you cheap drinks during happy hour. That they will pop around just to say hi. That they will text you in the middle of the night because the nightmares are just a little too scary. That they will come to your rescue and bring you cake.

I should've told you that you will find a great love. That even though you have resigned yourself to never being capable of being loved again, they will love you fiercely and without compromise. That they will inspire you to build dreams and chase unicorns because they're real. That you deserve love and happiness and all the fluffy feelings that make your knees weak and your heart full.

I should have told you that I love you. That it was impossible to say it too often.

There are so many things you need to do and life you must live – I wish I could remake the world for you so that I wouldn't need to write this letter. But roses are red and violets are blue. And one day, when you're all grown up, you'll have to write this letter for me too.

Chin up, big girl,

Zoey

~

Zoey Black is transgender woman living in Cape Town. She is a freelance actress, theatre production manager, content creator and blogger. Zoey is currently studying towards her Bachelor of Laws (LLB) at the University of South Africa. Follow her on Twitter and Instagram: @zoeyblackza

Glossary

You might read some words or phrases in this book that need some explaining. In those instances, these definitions will encourage better understanding.

ANC: African National Congress – the ruling party of South Africa.

Apartheid: Segregation in South Africa that was enforced until 1994.

Asexual: Someone who is not necessarily interested in sexual relations.

Bisexual: Loving both men and women, although a lot of bisexuals say they have claimed bisexual to mean **pansexual** – to love who you love regardless of gender and sexual characteristics.

Cishet: An abbreviation of 'cisheterosexual', which refers to people who are cisgender, as well as heterosexual.[32]

Cisgender: A person whose sense of gender and personal identity corresponds to the sex assigned at birth.

Coloured: Diverse group of people in South Africa descended largely from Cape slaves, the indigenous Khoisan population, and other people of African and Asian descent. Being also partly descended from European settlers, coloured people have been regarded as being of

---

32 Wang-Jones, Alhassoon, Hattrup, Ferdman, and Lowman. 2017. *Psychology of Sexual Orientation and Gender Diversity Development of Gender Identity Implicit Association Tests to Assess Attitudes Toward Transmen and Transwomen*. https://psycnet.apa.org/record/2017-01080-001. Last accessed 4 June 2019.

'mixed race'. The term was abused during apartheid to foster dominance over black people and play into racial hierarchy.[33]

Demi-gender: Individuals who feel a partial connection to a particular gender identity and do not fully subscribe to a particular gender. Examples of demi-gender identities include demi-girl, demi-boy and demi-androgyne.[34]

Femmephobia: Targets expressions of femininity which stray from the essentialist norms of what femininity is.

Gay: Men who are attracted to other men.

Gender Binary: The classification of sex and gender into two distinct, opposite and disconnected forms of masculine and feminine.[35]

Gender Fluid: A term used to describe someone who does not conform to gendered expectations or confine themselves to gendered boundaries in all aspects of being, including presentation.[36]

Gender Non-conforming: Relating to a person whose gender falls outside of the gender binary and a rebellion against the rigid boundaries set by it.[37]

---

33 Adhikari, M. 2006. Hope, Fear, Shame, Frustration: Continuity and Change in the Expression of Coloured Identity in White Supremacist South Africa, 1910–1994, *Journal of Southern African Studies*, 32(3): 467–487.

34 University of Massachusetts Amherst's Stonewall Center Allyship Handout. No date. https://www.umass.edu/stonewall/sites/default/files/documents/allyship_term_handout.pdf. Last accessed 4 June 2019.

35 Wikipedia. 2019. 'Gender Binary'. https://en.wikipedia.org/wiki/Gender_binary. Last accessed 4 June 2019.

36 American Psychological Association. 2015. Definitions Related to Sexual Orientation and Gender Diversity. https://www.apa.org/pi/lgbt/resources/sexuality-definitions.pdf. Last accessed 4 June 2019.

37 Kosciw, Greytak, Bartkiewicz, Boesen, & Palmer. 2012. *Key Terms and Concepts in Understanding Gender Diversity and Sexual Orientation among Students.* https://www.apa.org/pi/lgbt/programs/safe-supportive/lgbt/key-terms.pdf. Last accessed 28 June 2019.

Hetero-capitalism: The intersection of heterosexism and capitalism which combine to further oppress queer people. In other words, capitalism as a system which already oppresses marginalised people is made worse by the heterosexist nature of those who hold up the system.[38]

Heteronormative: Adhering to the sociocultural system that assumes the existence of only two sexes/genders; and which views sexual and social relations between a man and a woman as being natural and normal, with no other possibilities.

Heteropatriarchy: The belief that cisgender, heterosexual men are the natural born leaders in society.

Heterosexism: The discrimination of LGBTQIA+ people by heterosexuals based on the idea that heterosexuality is the social and cultural norm. It is also the belief that heterosexual people are superior to LGBTQIA+ people.[39]

Intersex: A broad term that can relate to various conditions. Many intersex people are born with ambiguous genitalia, or sex organs that are not clearly female or male.[40] 'Intersexuality is not a disorder.'[41]

Lesbian: Women who are attracted to other women.

LGBTQIA+ community: The acronym standing for lesbian, gay, bisexual, transgender, queer, intersex and asexual. The plus signifies that the alphabet is never-ending to make space for inclusivity.

---

38 Fraser, N. 1997. Heterosexism, Misrecognition, and Capitalism: A Response to Judith Butler. *Queer Transexions of Race, Nation, and Gender* p. 279-289 Duke University Press

39 Rainbow Resource Centre https://rainbowresourcecentre.org/files/12-11-Heterosexism.pdf Last accessed 5 June 2019.

40 Gross, S. No date. 'What is Intersex?' http://www.intersex.org.za/about-us/. Last accessed 5 July 2019.

41 Lee et al. 2013. *Your Hate Won't Change Us!* Cape Town, Triangle Project, p. 6.

Queer: An umbrella term that is used to describe a sexual orientation, gender identity or gender expression that does not conform to heteronormative societal norms.[42]

Moffie: At first a derogatory term aimed at gay men. Although a lot of gay men have reclaimed this word and use it with pride.

Non-binary: An identity that falls outside of the **gender binary**.

PAC: The Pan Africanist Congress of Azania is a South African Pan-Africanist movement that is now a political party, founded by an Africanist group which was led by Robert Sobukwe. Its origins come from a lack of consensus with the ANC after the freedom charter was adapted – Pan Africans within the ANC felt it was a betrayal of their struggles and broke away from the ANC to form the PAC.[43]

Pansexual: See under the expanded definition of **bisexual**.

Patriarchy: The belief that men are the natural born leaders in society.

Polyamorous: The term refers to the engagement in romantic or sexual relationships with more than one partner in which everyone involved in said relationships has given consent.[44]

Sex Worker: Adults who receive money or other forms of compensation in exchange for consensual sexual services, either regularly or occasionally. A sex worker can be male, female, intersex, woman, man or transgender.

Stabane: A Zulu word that was once used to describe an intersex person. It described intersexuality as a biological variation but is now used as a derogatory term for queer people.[45]

42 Amnesty International. 2015. *LGBTGQI Glossary*. https://www.amnestyusa.org/pdfs/AIUSA_Pride2015Glossary.pdf. Last accessed 4 June 2019.

43 South African History Online, https://www.sahistory.org.za/article/pan-africanist-congress-pac. Last accessed 4 June 2019.

44 Balzarini, R.N. 2017. Perceptions of primary and secondary relationships in polyamory. *PLOS ONE*, 12(5).

45 Lock Swarr, A. 2019. Stabane. Intersexuality, and Same-Sex Relationships in South Africa. *Feminist Studies*, 35(3): 524–548

Transphobia: Irrational fear or hostility towards trans people.

Transgender: A person whose gender identity does not match that typically associated with their biological sex, or which was assigned to them at birth.[46] Being transgender does not imply any particular sexual orientation or that any form of reassignment surgery is required.

Womxn: A woman. (Used, especially in intersectional feminism, as an alternative spelling to avoid the suggestion of sexism perceived in the sequences *m-a-n* and *m-e-n*, and to be inclusive of trans and non-binary women.)[47]

46 Tamale, S. (Ed). 2011. *African Sexualities: A Reader*. Pambazuka Press: Cape Town, Dakar, Nairobi and Oxford.

47 Dictionary.com. 'Womxn'. https://www.dictionary.com/browse/womxn. Last accessed 4 June 2019.

Resources

Podcasts

AfroQueer https://afroqueerpodcast.com

Brothaspeak https://www.brothaspeakpod.net

LGBTQ&A https://www.lgbtqpodcast.com

QueerWOC https://queerwoc.com

Tea with Queen and J. https://soundcloud.com/tea-with-queen-and-j

The Wildness with Tiff and Manda https://soundcloud.com/thewildness-
tiffandmanda

Books and Articles

Feminism meets Queer Theory by Elizabeth Weed and Naomi Schor (Eds.)

Queer Africa 2 by Makhosazana Xaba and Karen Martin (Eds.)

Queer in Africa: LGBTQI Identities, Citizenship, and Activism by Zethu
Matebeni, Surya Monro and Vasu Reddy

What does the Q mean? Including queer voices in qualitative research
by Denise L. Levy & Corey W. Johnson https://doi.org/10.1177/
1473325011400485

Why the Queer Community Needs to Talk About Mental Health by Rachel
Charlene Lewis https://www.pride.com/identities/2019/4/20/why-queer-
community-needs-talk-about-mental-health

*Sad, Brown, And Gay: Let's Talk About Queer and Trans Mental Health in
The South Asian Diaspora* by Aditi Natasha Kini https://www.intomore.
com/impact/sad-brown-and-gay-lets-talk-about-queer-and-trans-
mental-health-in-the-south-asian-diaspora

Why We Must Protect Sex Workers at All Costs During The #MeToo Era by Neesha Powell https://everydayfeminism.com/2018/01/sex-workers-and-me-too

What Does "Queer" Mean? 5 Things to Know About The Q In LGBTQ by Marissa Higgins https://www.bustle.com/articles/175470-what-does-queer-mean-5-things-to-know-about-the-q-in-lgbtq

Coming Out As Queer Is Even More Complicated For A Fat Person by Charlotte Morabito https://everydayfeminism.com/author/charlottem

The Missing Colors of the Rainbow: Black Queer Resistance by Elena Kiesling

Womxn's and nonbinary activists' contribution to the RhodesMustFall and FeesMustFall student movements: 2015 and 2016. Barbara Boswell, Simamkele Dlakavu and Sandy Ndelu https://www.tandfonline.com/doi/full/10.1080/10130950.2017.1394693

Feminist Reflections on the Rhodes Must Fall Movement by Kealeboga Ramaru http://www.agi.ac.za/sites/default/files/image_tool/images/429/feminist_africa_journals/archive/22/fa22_standpoint_1.pdf

Organisations

Gay and Lesbian Memory in Action https://gala.co.za

Gay and Lesbian Network https://gaylesbian.org.za

Gender Dynamix https://www.genderdynamix.org.za

Global Interfaith Network http://www.gin-ssogie.org

Health4Men https://www.health4men.co.za

Iranti http://iranti-org.co.za

LGBT+ Forum http://www.lgbtforum.org

Love Not Hate http://www.lovenothate.org.za

Rape Crisis Cape Town http://rapecrisis.org.za

OUT https://www.out.org.za

Oxfam South Africa https://www.oxfam.org.za

Pride Shelter Trust https://www.prideshceltertrust.com

Same Love Toti http://pflagsouthafrica.org

Sex Workers Education and Advocacy Taskforce http://www.sweat.org.za

Sonke Gender Justice https://genderjustice.org.za

Triangle Project https://triangle.org.za

Women's Legal Centre http://wlce.co.za

Bibliography

Adhikari, M. 2006. Hope, Fear, Shame, Frustration: Continuity and Change in the Expression of Coloured Identity in White Supremacist South Africa, 1910–1994, *Journal of Southern African Studies*, 32(3): 467–487.

Adkins, L. & Skeggs, B. (Eds.). 2004. *Feminism after Bourdieu*. Blackwell Publishing, Malden: Oxford, UK.

Ahmed, S. 2004. Affective Economies. *Social Text*, *22*(2): 117–139.

American Psychological Association. 2015. *Definitions Related to Sexual Orientation and Gender Diversity*. https://www.apa.org/pi/lgbt/resources/sexuality-definitions.pdf. Last accessed 4 June 2019.

Amnesty International. 2015. *LGBTQI Glossary*. https://www.amnestyusa.org/pdfs/AIUSA_Pride2015Glossary.pdf. Last accessed 4 June 2019.

Animashaun, A. & Iradukunda, I. & Kimutai, T. & Muranda, T. & Speaks, S. (Eds.). 2016. *Walking the Tightrope: Poetry and Prose by LGBTQ Writers from Africa*. Tincture/Lethe Press: New Jersey.

Ashall, W. 2004. Masculine Domination: Investing in Gender? *Studies in Social and Political Thought*, 9(1): 21–39.

Balzarini, R.N. 2017. Perceptions of primary and secondary relationships in polyamory. *PLOS ONE*, 12(5).

Blaira, K. L. & Hoskins, R. A. 2014. Experiences of femme identity: Coming out, invisibility and femmephobia. *Psychology and Sexuality*, 6(3), Department of Psychology, University of Utah, Salt Lake City, USA.

Boswell, B. & Dlakavu S. & Ndelu, S. 2017. Womxn's and nonbinary activists' contribution to the RhodesMustFall and FeesMustFall student movements: 2015 and 2016. Cape Town. https://www.tandfonline.com/doi/full/10.1080/10130950.2017.1394693 Last accessed 4 June 2019.

Bourdieu, P. (1996). On the Family as a Realized Category. *Theory, Culture & Society*, *13*(3): 19–26.

Bourdieu, P. & Johnson, R. 1993. *The Field of Cultural Production: Essays on Art and Literature*. Columbia University Press: New York.

Bourdieu, P. 1986. The forms of capital. In J. Richardson (Ed.) *Handbook of Theory and Research for the Sociology of Education,* p. 241–258. Greenwood: New York.

Butler, J. 1990. *Gender Trouble: Feminism and the Subversion of Identity*. Routledge: New York.

Coleman, J. S. 1990. *Foundations of Social Theory*. Belknap Press of Harvard University Press: Cambridge, Massachusetts.

Coyote, I. & Sharman, Z. (Eds.). 2011. *Persistence: All Ways Butch and Femme*. Arsenal Pulp Press: Vancouver.

Dictionary.com. 'Womxn'. https://www.dictionary.com/browse/womxn. Last accessed 4 June 2019.

Garland-Thomson, R. 1997. *Extraordinary Bodies: Figuring Physical Disability in American Culture and Literature*. Columbia University Press: New York.

Goffman, E. 1963. *Stigma: Notes on the Management of Spoiled Identity*. Penguin: London.

Gross, S. No date. 'What is Intersex?' http://www.intersex.org.za/about-us/ Last accessed 5 July 2019.

Halperin, D. 1997. *Saint Foucault: Towards a Gay Hagiography*. Oxford University Press: Oxford.

Higgins, M. 2016. What Does "Queer" Mean? 5 Things To Know About The Q In LGBTQ https://www.bustle.com/articles/175470-what-doesqueer-mean-5-things-to-know-about-the-q-in-lgbtq Last accessed 4 June 2019.

Fanon, F. 1956. *Black Skin, White Masks*. Pluto-Press: London.

Foucault, M. 1978. *The History of Sexuality* (1st American ed). Pantheon Books: New York.

Foucault, M. 1977. *Discipline and Punish: The Birth of the Prison*. Vintage Books: New York.

Foucault, M. 1982. *The Archaeology of Knowledge*. Pantheon Books: New York.

Foucault, M. 1991. *Discipline and Punish: The Birth of the Prison*. Penguin: London.

Fraser, N. 1997. Heterosexism, Misrecognition, and Capitalism: A Response to Judith Butler. *Queer Transexions of Race, Nation, and Gender*. Duke University Press: 279–289.

Kiesling, E. 2017. The Missing Colors of the Rainbow: Black Queer Resistance. European Association for American Studies. USA.

Kini, A. 2018. Sad, Brown, And Gay: c. https://www.intomore.com/impact/sad-brown-and-gay-lets-talk-about-queer-and-transmental-health-in-the-south-asian-diaspora Last accessed 4 June 2019.

Kosciw, Greytak, Bartkiewicz, Boesen, & Palmer. 2012. *Key Terms and Concepts in Understanding Gender Diversity and Sexual Orientation among Students*.

Lee, P.W.Y., Lynch, I. and Clayton, M. 2013. *Your Hate Won't Change Us! Resisting homophobic and transphobic violence as forms of patriarchal social control*. Triangle Project. Cape Town. p. 6.

Levy, D. L., & Johnson, C. W. (2012). What does the Q mean? Including queer voices in qualitative research. *Qualitative Social Work*, 11(2): 130–140.

Lewis, R. 2019. Why the Queer Community Needs to Talk About Mental Health https://www.pride.com/identities/2019/4/20/why-queer-community-needs-talk-about-mental-health Last accessed 4 June 2019.

Lock Swarr, A. 2019. Stabane. Intersexuality, and Same-Sex Relationships in South Africa. *Feminist Studies*, 35(3): 524–548.

Powell, N. 2018. Why We Must Protect Sex Workers at All Costs

During The #MeToo Era https://everydayfeminism.com/2018/01/sex-workersand-me-too

Morabito, C. 2017. Coming Out As Queer Is Even More Complicated For A Fat Person https://everydayfeminism.com/2017/09/queer-fat-personcomplicated. Last accessed 4 June 2019.

Matebeni, Z. & Monro, S. & Reddy, V. (Eds.) 2017. *Queer in Africa: LGBTQI Identities, Citizenship, and Activism*. Routledge: UK.

Muñoz, J. E. 2009. *Cruising Utopia: The Then and There of Queer Futurity*. New York University Press: New York.

Nkumane, Z. 2018. Daily moments of loneliness, *Mail & Guardian*, https://mg.co.za/article/2018-10-12-00-daily-moments-of-loneliness. Last accessed 5 June 2019.

Onorato, R. S. & Turner, J. C. 2004. Fluidity in the self-concept: the shift from personal to social identity. *European Journal of Social Psychology*, 34(3): 257–278.

Puwar, N. 2004. *Space Invaders: Race, Gender and Bodies Out of Place*. Oxford: New York.

Rainbow Resource Centre https://rainbowresourcecentre.org/files/12-11-Heterosexism.pdf Last accessed 5 June 2019

Ramaru, K. 2017. Feminist Reflections on the Rhodes Must Fall Movement. Cape Town. http://www.agi.ac.za/sites/default/files/image_tool/images/429/feminist_africa_journals/archive/22/fa22_standpoint_1.pdf Last accessed 5 June

Rumi, J. 1676. *Rumi's Shams of Tabriz* (Classics of World Spirituality). Vega Books.

South African History Online, https://www.sahistory.org.za/article/panafricanist-congress-pac. Last accessed 4 June 2019.

Tamale, S. (Ed.). 2011. *African Sexualities: A Reader*. Pambazuka Press: Cape Town, Dakar, Nairobi and Oxford.

Taormino, T. 5 October 1999. Of Butches, Kings, and Masculinity. Village Voice. http://www.villagevoice.com/1999-10-05/columns/of-butches-kings-andmasculinity. Archived, no longer available.

University of Massachusetts Amherst's Stonewall Center Allyship Handout. No date. https://www.umass.edu/stonewall/sites/default/files/documents/allyship_term_handout.pdf. Last accessed 4 June 2019.

Wang-Jones, Alhassoon, Hattrup, Ferdman, & Lowman. 2017. Development of gender identity implicit association tests to assess attitudes toward transmen and transwomen. *Psychology of Sexual Orientation and Gender Diversity.* https://psycnet.apa.org/record/2017-01080-001. Last accessed 4 June 2019.

Wikipedia. 2019. 'Gender Binary'. https://en.wikipedia.org/wiki/Gender_binary. Last accessed 4 June 2019.

Wild Gender. 7 May 2012. http://wildgender.com/. Last accessed 5 June 2019.

Weed, E. 1997. *Feminism meets Queer Theory.* Indiana University Press: Chicago.

Xaba, M. & Martin, K. 2017. *Queer Africa 2: New Stories.* MaThoko: South Africa.

Acknowledgements

Compiling a book of essays is never easy. There are late nights crying because an essay was not submitted on time and there are negotiations between contributor, compiler and editor regarding edits and style. And then suddenly, after all the back and forth and all the rush, there comes a time when everyone is happy, the book goes to print, and we feel this renewed sense of possibility through collaboration.

They Called Me Queer would not have been possible without our publisher, Kwela Books, who trusted us with curating the book and its contributors. We were blessed to have Na'eemah Masoet on our team. To our editor, Kelly Smith, who worked overtime to ensure that the book looks and reads perfectly – we thank you. To all of our contributors – Andiswa Mkosi, Carl Collison, Chase Rhys, Clio Koopman, Craig Lucas, Gulam Petersen, Haji Mohamed Dawjee, Jamil F Khan, Janine Adams, Katlego K. Kolanyane-Kesupile, Khanya Kemani, Lester Walbrugh, Ling Sheperd, Luh Maquba, Lwando Scott, Lyle Lackay, Maneo Mohale, Mary Hames, Neo Baepi, Nicole Adams, Noluvuyo Zaza, Qondiswa James, Sandrine Mpazayabo, Shelley Barry, Sizakele Phohleli, Tiffany Kagure Mugo, Wanelisa Xaba and Zoey Black – your contributions made us cry, made us think, made us process, and made us recognise once more why story-telling is important and why we should ensure that queer people of colour's voices are centred, understood and amplified.

Thank you to the team behind *She Called Me Woman: Nigeria's Queer Women Speak*, the book that propelled us to create a South African version, who so graciously and excitedly allowed us to continue their work in any way that we envisioned. A special thank you to Kealeboga Ramaru for assisting with compiling the resources list and to Clio Koopman for assisting with compiling the glossary page. A special thank you to GALA for our cover image of Piper Laurie from their Kewpie Exhibition. Ismail Hanif, better known as Piper Laurie, was a well-known character from District Six, Cape Town. A talented dancer and hairdresser, Piper worked and travelled around southern Africa for ten years, but for most of her life was based in District Six, and later in Mitchells Plain. Laurie was part of a queer community that was highly visible and integrated into the broader community, representing an important part of the social fabric and culture of District Six. Members of this queer community sometimes identified as gay men and sometimes identified as women. Laurie and her contemporaries generally used feminine pronouns in referring to each other and whilst they may not necessarily have identified as queer, the intentional blurring of the gender binary can be viewed as queer. To everyone who assisted in the process and to everyone who will be assisting us in the process for our next book – we thank you.

Queerly yours,
Kim Windvogel and Kelly-Eve Koopman